LOFTING

ALLAN H. VAITSES

INTERNATIONAL MARINE PUBLISHING COMPANY
Camden, Maine

Plans of *Araminta* in Chapter 5 are published with the permission of Muriel Vaughn. Some of these plans are also included in *Sensible Cruising Designs,* by L. Francis Herreshoff, published in 1973 by International Marine Publishing Company.

©1980
by International Marine Publishing Company
Library of Congress Catalog Card Number 78-75110
International Standard Book Number 0-87742-113-7
Typeset by A & B Typesetters, Inc., Concord, New Hampshire
Printed and spiral-bound by The Alpine Press, Stoughton, Massachusetts

Published by International Marine Publishing Company
21 Elm Street, Camden, Maine 04843

Third printing, 1982

Contents

Introduction

For those readers who have no background in lofting, I thought it would be good to start with the complete lofting of a simple skiff. For others who may be squeezed for time or space, or have a project in mind that doesn't need much lofting, I'll follow with directions on how to set it up using minimum lofting techniques. Perhaps this will save builders from a degree of frustration, a lot of wading through intricacies they don't yet feel a need for, or even from chucking this book aside. As we go along, I'll introduce tools and methods, rather than pack these into textbook-like chapters that nobody would read. Meanwhile, I'm sure the fellow with an in-depth interest will sail right through and will be waiting for us further on.

In later chapters we will get into more involved projects, and parts and details that, in a lifetime of boatbuilding, I have found it useful to loft. We will have a look at keels, decks, sterns, as well as frames, floors, and other parts. We will have to take another look at some of these parts because of the different treatment they require to loft and set up efficiently in the newer boatbuilding methods. Because lofting for one-off fiberglass and lofting for tooling have become important facets of the trade, having their own special requirements, I will devote a chapter to these.

Complete coverage or exhaustive knowledge is not claimed by any means. The subject is as broad as the range of possible shapes and constructions and as deep as the detail to which you carry the lofting. The best way to get a grasp on lofting is to actually do it.

This reality is reflected in the topical nature of this book, where the lofting procedures of three specific boats—representing three boat types—are followed through. From the descriptions of these lofting procedures, you should get a good grasp on overall lofting procedures that are applicable to all boats. However, you will also find that some of the techniques explained might apply only when certain situations are encountered and won't apply in all cases. This is why, as in everything, experience is the best teacher in lofting.

I once watched from the respectful distance of a new hire in a Navy yard loft as the top lofting and drafting brass huddled over a submarine's lines on the floor working out the lofting of a sea chest of 1-inch steel. This chest was to be folded in one piece like a pasteboard box (to minimize welded joints, I suppose). And it was to come out of the folding process with four edges fitting against the hull's skin. That was when I decided that lofting has plenty of challenge if enough is asked of it. That the effort can be worthwhile was dramatized by that steel box whose edges could never have been profiled as efficiently as when a true template was drawn in the first place.

Here is one more remark on lofting: rather than lose someone to boatbuilding because lofting really turns him off, it should be mentioned that there are companies that will deliver full-size lofting of any plan, enabling one to get right into building his boat. At the same time, a boatbuilder with lofting experience is bound to be a cut above the chap with no experience when it comes to understanding what he's building, how it got that way from a few lines on paper, and how to find his way around when he's looking at boat plans. As the teachers used to tell us in school about Latin and algebra, "It's good for you, even if you never have to use it."

1 / Lofting, How Much?

Lofting, simply put, is the process of drawing the lines of a boat and some of its parts full size to get the shapes and patterns needed to build it. If you were building a straight-sided, flat-bottomed scow, you could simply lay off the dimensions on lumber or steel, cut out the pieces, and fasten them up in place on a level bed. But when the vessel—whether dinghy or ship—is a shapely thing, with constantly changing curves, there is just no way to get started without drawing and making up a number of full-size skeletal pieces on which to bend the rest of her. You sometimes don't need much, but you must have something. Only the chap chopping a dugout from a log might proceed with no lofting. But if he has not been born and brought up with the art, he too will be more efficient if he has some templates and battens to guide and fair his work. Even lines produced by the most skilled designer can benefit from the fairing that comes with drawing the lines full size.

Wooden battens are the traditional tools for fairing lines. When using them to fair a designer's lines, the builder should keep in mind this maxim: *"A fair line supersedes any given measurement."* That's the secret of good lofting, and of good boatbuilding too, as opposed to simply blowing up the plans.

The first problem with lofting is deciding how much of it to do on a given boat. Should you simply draw the profile and a few stations, pick up the backbone and a few moulds, and get on with the building? Or should you kneel on the loft floor day after day drawing the entire plan, fairing and checking it; developing the expanded transom pattern; drawing each timber in the keel assembly; defining the rabbet, back rabbet, bearding line, and scarfs; and drawing in knees, deadwood, rudder, propeller aperture, shaft log, engine beds, stringers, floor timbers, mast steps, bulkheads, bulwarks, fiddlehead, decks, cockpit, and houses? Many high-quality craft have been built using either of these approaches—and so have many "clunkers."

Unfortunately, the potential for perfection has to be shared with the designer and the boatbuilding crew. The loftsman cannot make a good boat from a bad design, nor can he insure against sloppy workmanship. What he can do is to guarantee that the craft is an accurate representation of the plan, fair her lines, and lay out her most important members in their proper locations, shapes, and dimensions. It is pure joy to build on lofting that has been done with accuracy and a good eye and picked up with proper markings and identification. This is when everything seems to fall into place, and you know you can get out the plans or lofting years later and be sure that this is exactly how she is, to the fraction of an inch.

In that sense, it is hard to say that any amount of lofting is wasted. Yet different shapes, sizes, types of construction, and degrees of complexity in craft certainly call for a different amount of lofting to get a suitable working basis. For instance, in a flat-transomed V-bottomed boat that is to be built of plywood or steel, there are only three important long lines to fair in two views before you can pick up the makings of a decently fair hull.

A lapstrake hull of modest size also requires minimal lofting when planked over moulds rather than frames. In this case, there is little reason to loft, pick up, and set up more than the backbone and a few rather widely spaced station moulds because the planking will tend to fair the hull. Bulkheads, frames, and floors can be fitted to the hull's inside and scribed to all of the planking at once. If the vessel is double-ended and the stem and sternpost are left unrabbeted, the lofting will be further simplified. These members can be finished off later with an outer or "false" stem, making it unnecessary to loft the rabbet and bearding lines. Due to its minimal lofting needs and the ease of fitting the planks once you get the "hang" of them, lapstrake construction is still by far the fastest and easiest way to build a shapely wooden hull.

On the other hand, if you wish to build a massive vessel with sawn frames, you will save an enormous number of man-hours if you loft and pick up patterns of every bit of her keel assembly, frames, and floors, and every rabbet, scarf, and bevel. Despite the power tools we have today, fitting and fairing such heavy stock is slow, arduous work. In this case, it really pays off to do a thorough job of lofting so that you can cut each member just right the first time.

Racing sailboats built to various rating rules require a full lofting job and meticulous measurement. The lines must be held at critical points where the designer is striving for all the boat he can get, yet cannot exceed certain dimensions lest the vessel be rated higher, or actually not measure into her class. I do not find it particularly inspiring to loft racers whose lines are distorted for the sake of measurement. In fact, it is frustrating to find myself using as many picks on one side of a batten as on the other to force it into curves that may be as designed, but that could hardly be called sweeping, and never beautiful. All you can do is look at such jobs as a challenge—and they certainly are more so than a set of sweet and easy lines that fall neatly into place and fill you so full of admiration that you can't wait to run the next one.

Lofting for fiberglass boats can be either very involved or very simple. If the boat is to be built one-off, you don't need a very involved lofting job to build the framework most methods require. Nor is it of much use to be over-solicitous about tiny discrepancies in fairing and checking, since the framework construction will give you another chance to fair the lines as you fit the ribbands onto or into the moulds. Also, as you build up the layers of fiberglass on the PVC foam, C-Flex, Stretch-Mesh, or other starting material, you will be building up more unfairness than there is in any decent job of lofting. It's the nature of a plastic material to get thinned out here and thickened there as you brush, roll, squeegee, or trowel it. This goes for plastering ferrocement boats, too. The only way you can get real accuracy in a boat built up on the outside with plastic materials is to pick up templates and periodically check out the shape. But, in most cases you should be satisfied to bring your one-off hull to the fairest and smoothest condition you can by grinding down high spots and filling in the lows and topping it off with a slick paint or gelcoat job. This will be a mean enough task without worrying about being a bit over or a bit under the designed lines.

It is quite another matter when you loft a prototype or a plug on which tooling will be made for fiberglass production boats. Good sense tells you that the utmost care in lofting is none too much when the form of hundreds of potential boats is at stake. Unfortunately you see many misshapen boats these days that have obviously resulted from bad tooling. Such tooling would have to be the product of indifferent lofting, possibly aided and abetted by sloppy plug building (unless it is the result of no lofting or plug building at all). Sometimes models are born by "grabbing" molds off existing boats that haven't been carefully checked or faired before the act.

How much lofting you need to do, then, is related to how much quality and timesaving in building is needed or wanted in the job at hand. But there is one more important factor: the proficiency of the designer of the boat in connection with the nature of the plans. If the designer is a good and accurate draftsman, the boat you build from a skimpy lofting job could still be as sweet and fair as one you lofted to the nth degree from a poorly conceived and faired lines plan.

I remember feeling a little let down when, after years of carefully lofting each custom boat I built, I read a remark by L. Francis Herreshoff that it was not really necessary to draw all the long lines of a boat and fair them: one could just draw the profile and the body plan, pick up the backbone and moulds of the stations, and go ahead with the building. But then, thinking back, I realized that his plans and those of other excellent designers (and/or draftsmen, because you never know in the big design offices who actually drew and faired the lines plan or took off the table of offsets) had needed very little fairing or correction. Also, it was L. Francis' habit to draw the stem, keel assembly, and other important members in great detail to a larger scale than the other plans, so that one might dare to make up the pieces and rabbet and bevel them from the dimensions given.

As usual, L. Francis was right—at least within the context of reassuring an amateur builder, who might be handy with tools but leery of lofting—that a boat built with minimal lofting could come out just as well as one that is lofted completely. As one example, it just happens that in Herreshoff's *Nereia* design there is a slight flat place in the underbody a little aft of amidships where you need to let the batten go a bit. But I have seen people do a full job of lofting *Nereia* and then pick her up and build her so that she retains this unfairness absolutely intact. This is pretty good proof that a full job of lofting is no guarantee of perfection.

At the same time, a careful builder with a good eye who has done only the minimum amount of lofting necessary might notice such an instance of unfairness in his ribbands, or while planking, and get rid of it. It is even possible that, without noticing a particular spot as being unfair, one might eradicate it more or less automatically by following proper building procedures. In a boat with steam-bent frames like *Nereia*, the proper procedure is to plank from the keel up rather than to plank down from the sheerstrake and up from the keel at the same time. If the boat is planked from the keel up, the frames can creep a little to accommodate the planking as it tries to lie fair.

So let's just say that there's more to lofting than simply drawing every line in the plan full size, and that there's more to boatbuilding than looking down our noses at anyone who doesn't draw every line.

2 / Lofting a Flat-Bottomed Skiff

For a long, long time it has been recognized that the easiest way to start building a boat or ship is to draw her profile and a number of athwartship sections full size, pick them up in solid form, and set them up. For as long, these have been the primary tasks of the loftsman. To illustrate this procedure in a rather simplified fashion, in this chapter we shall have a look at what it takes to loft a 12-foot, flat-bottomed, straight-sided skiff.

What Defines a Vessel's Shape

The shape of this 12-foot skiff can be given by five parts; these five parts—stem, transom mould, and three station moulds—are all you need to get started on her. This assembly defines the shape of the boat so well that whenever its parts are set up the same distance apart and at the same heights and angles relative to a horizontal plane, it will always result in the same boat. Her profile is established at the rail and bottom on each piece and is embodied at the ends by the stem and transom, while the station moulds establish the shape of the body in between. To create these parts, then, is the basic goal of lofting.

A similar set of basic parts will define the shape of any hull, whether it be a ship, dinghy, submarine, or hydroplane.

These shape-defining parts need only be modified as to shape and number for each different vessel. For example, if this skiff were longer, you might need moulds at more stations along her length, or if she were more shapely, she might need more closely spaced moulds to form the curves, especially near the ends. On the other hand, some boats can be built around a single midship station mould, as in a small pram or garvey.

Anyway, the most useful way to express the shape of a boat is in terms of its profile and these athwartship slices known as sections. We can and will slice a boat in other ways: horizontally to get waterlines, vertically lengthwise to get buttock lines, and lengthwise at an angle to get diagonals. We will be taking up these "long lines" as we go along, but a certain number of sections are the only lines besides the profile that you *must* have to build a vessel. Coincidentally, after the profile, sections also seem to be the most easily appreciated lines, perhaps because they give us an end view of a boat's shape.

A common practice of designer-builders years ago was to draw each half-section on its station line in the profile drawing. This was, and still is, a good shorthand expression of a vessel's shape: the section can be simply drawn in between the bottom of the keel at the station line and a horizontal extension of the point where the sheer and station lines intersect.

You can usually assume that such a lines plan was taken off either an existing boat or off a carved builder's model. After an old-time designer-builder had thoughtfully shaped and carefully faired his model, he could put its shape on paper by simply tracing around its profile, marking off some stations, and transferring

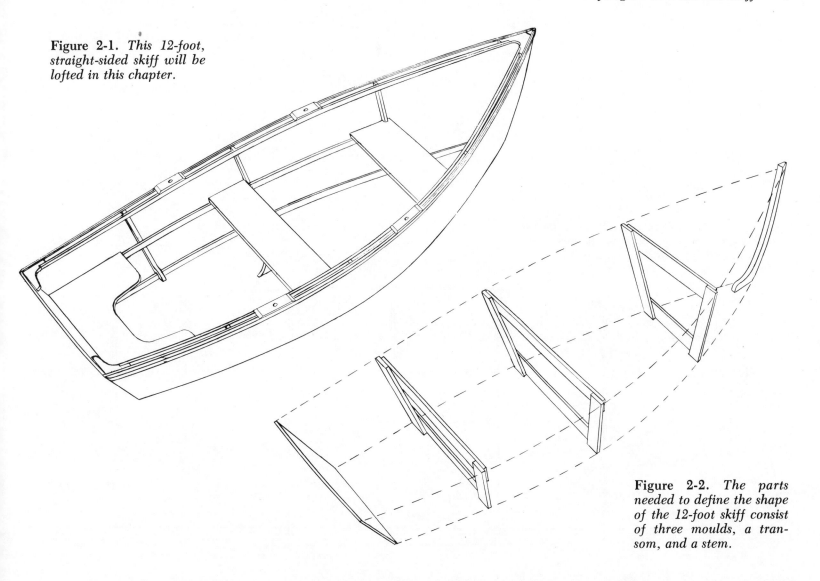

Figure 2-1. *This 12-foot, straight-sided skiff will be lofted in this chapter.*

Figure 2-2. *The parts needed to define the shape of the 12-foot skiff consist of three moulds, a transom, and a stem.*

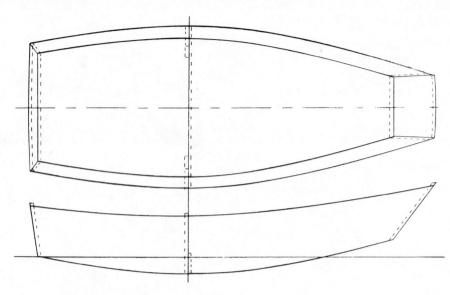

Right: Figure 2-3. *A hull with little shape needs few pieces to define its shape.*

Figure 2-4. *A shapely hull such as the double-ender shown below requires numerous moulds to define its shape.*

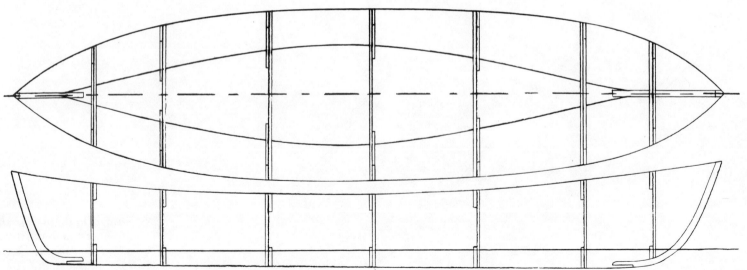

the sectional shapes of the stations from model to drawing. The transfer was made by making saw cuts in the model and slipping in cards on which to trace the stations or by bending a strip of lead around the model. Nathanael Herreshoff used a pantograph to transfer the sections of his models to construction drawings, and he took off the offsets with a machine that "read" the half-breadths and heights directly from the model for any point on the hull.

Building from model, to loft, to boat is efficient, and it can yield a fine boat. The problem with this method for modern designers is that it doesn't yield a complete lines plan that can be mailed to bidders, builders, prospective owners, and publications. Interiors and other details cannot be shown, and all the calculations and comparisons related to performance and ratings cannot be undertaken. Therefore, paper plans are now used by all designers except for the few remaining old-time designer-builders.

In this method, the designer does not carve a model but creates

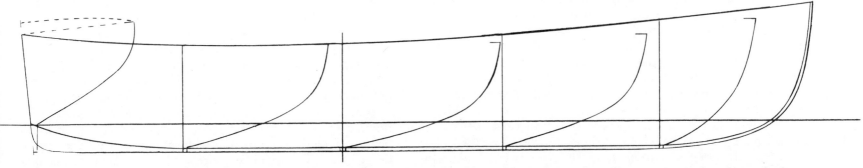

Above: Figure 2-5. *Designer-builders used this simple method to present on paper the shape of their models.* **Below: Figure 2-6.** *In*

paper plans, the vessel's shape is shown in a body plan, which consists of all the sections grouped around a common centerline.

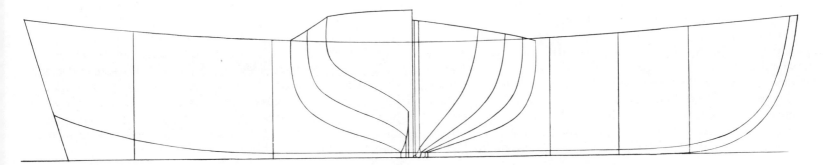

his design directly on paper. With no three-dimensional form to use as a basis and for checking fairness, the designer must draw a multiplicity of lines that cross-check each other in the three different views—profile, half-breadth, and athwartships—in which the lines are presented. The resulting plan gives a far clearer indication of the vessel's shape than does the sketchy builder's half model type of plan. A comparison between the treatment of the sections in the two methods proves the point. Instead of spreading out the sections over the length of the profile, the original lines plan arranges them into a body plan centered around the midship station of the profile, with the forward sections on the right and the aft sections on the left. This shows a boat's form from the ends as it is seen to change in a stepped sort of fashion and gives a good impression of a boat's shape. This arrangement is also the same compact form in which the sections are drawn full size; it saves space and it saves the loftsman the trouble of having to move about with his gear when picking the sections up as moulds.

How a boat's plans are presented and in what detail often depends on whom she is being designed for. Recalling the 12-foot skiff, if the designer is trying to make it easy to build her, as he might if he were publishing a "how to build" article or book, he would show some dimensioned plans of the parts and a setting-up diagram like that shown in Figure 2–7. With a plan like this, lofting would amount to little more than measuring, cutting, and assembling the five parts shown in Figure 2–2.

However, if the designer is not telling an amateur, or anyone in particular, how to build the boat, his plan might be as cryptic as a simple lines plan. (*See* Figure 2–8.) Don't worry, there's no question that any boat can be built with only this much information. Note that the skeletal outlines of the minimal five parts are there plus the entire profile. All you have to do is measure everything with a scale rule using the scale given and transfer it to a full-size drawing. Even if a scale is not given or if a plan is not to the par-

ticular scale that you would like to build to, you can make your own scale and loft the boat to the given length or to a length that you choose.

By way of illustration, there is a line of catboats in three sizes currently being produced that were all lofted from the same tattered lines plan of a really nice, old design. One size was lofted to the scale of the plan; the others were lofted at different scales, according to the desired length. In most models, a change in size by a few feet will not make much difference; in this case, the catboats seem to suffer nothing noticeable when scaled down to 14 feet and up to 25 feet from the original 18 feet.

Not all size changes are the same, however. Due to the different magnitudes by which certain dimensions change relative to others as the scale is changed, it is better to scale a plan up rather than to scale it down. The expanded boat is relatively more powerful, for its displacement increases with the cube of its dimensions while its sail area increases only with the square of the dimensions. This means that a boat cannot be scaled up too much before the increase in the displacement outpaces the increase in the sail plan. There will therefore need to be some adjustment of such a vessel's driving force, whether it be sail or power. If no such adjustment is undertaken, though, the boat will just be underpowered—not necessarily a bad situation. What is more serious about scaling down too much is that the greatly decreased displacement may render the boat too unstable to carry its relatively bigger rig or engine. In fact, even the crew can become too much of a burden for a very small scaled-down craft.

One good trick to compensate for the cubic increase or decrease in displacement is to stretch or compress the station spacing while holding the width constant. My boatyard built some pretty fine bigger or smaller sisterships by simply putting in or taking out a chunk in the middle of the design. When undertaking such an operation, it certainly helps to be a loftsman.

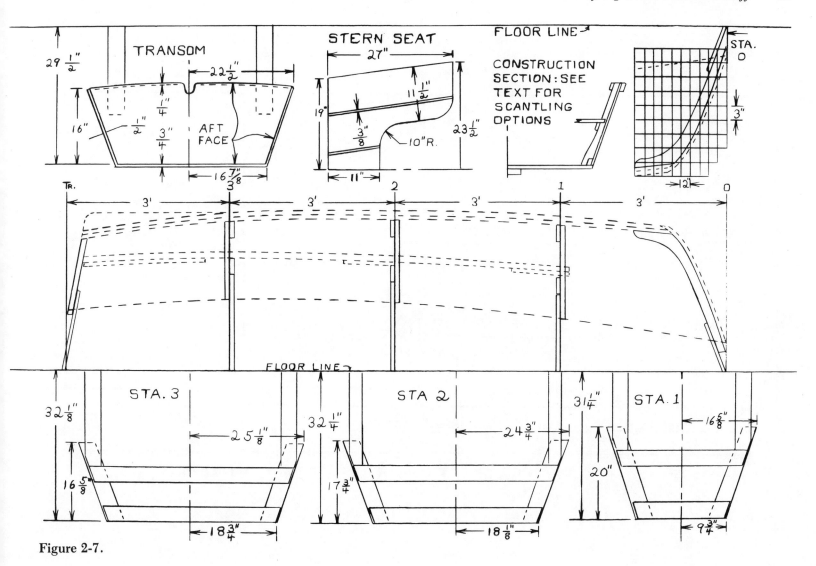

Figure 2-7.

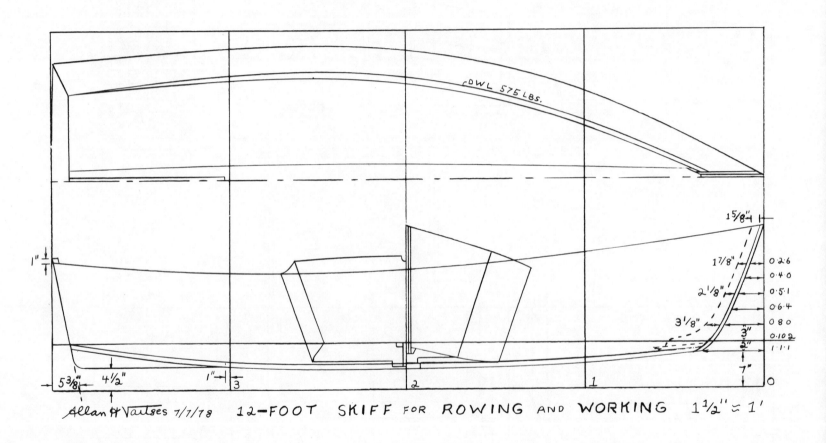

DWL 575 LBS.

1⅝"

1⅞"   0·2·6
             0·4·0
2⅛"   0·5·1
             0·6·4
3⅛"   0·8·0
          3" 0·10·2
          2" 1·1·1
          7"

1"

5⅜" 4½"   1" 3

2

1

0

Allan H Vaitses 7/7/78   12-FOOT SKIFF FOR ROWING AND WORKING   1½" ≃ 1'

Figure 2-8.

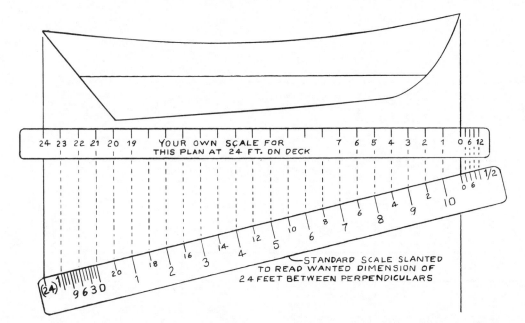

Figure 2-9.

Making your own scale for lofting a plan that doesn't fit a standard scale is simple. Extend two parallel lines perpendicular to a known or wanted dimension on the plan. Angle a rule having the scale closest to the desired dimension across the parallels until it reads that dimension and draw more parallels through the markings of the rule. When these are extended to a line that is perpendicular to the parallels, the parallels will mark it off into the scale units needed to loft the boat that size.

Naturally, a designer would not intentionally put you through an exercise like the above. He will almost always send you a plan to a standard scale and will measure the plan himself and provide you with a table of offsets. The table of offsets is simply an expression of the hull's shape using measurements taken from the hull lines at certain points where they intersect lines of reference. All measurements are given as heights or widths as they relate to some line used as a standard, which is usually termed the baseline. The measurements are commonly expressed in feet, inches, and eighths of inches, with the entries followed by a plus or minus sign to indicate when the measurement doesn't fall on the eighth inch. In the table, then, one foot four-and-one-quarter inches would read 1-4-2. One foot four-and-five-sixteenths inches might read either 1-4-2(+) or 1-4-3(−). To determine which of these it really is takes an awfully good eye, especially when reading a plan where an inch or less equals one foot.

Like the lines plan, a good table of offsets may provide enough information in itself to loft the boat. It should, for making up a table of offsets is an actual step in the process of scaling the lines in order to draw them full size. The only information that might be missing would be those dimensions that the designer might, for reasons of clarity or brevity, decide to show in place on the lines

12-FOOT SKIFF FOR ROWING AND WORKING

TABLE OF OFFSETS ~ TO OUTSIDE OF PLANKING

Allan H. Vaitses 7/7/78		OFFSETS IN FEET, INCHES AND EIGHTHS				
		BOW	STA 1	STA 2	STA 3	TRANS
HEIGHTS	SHEER	2-8-0	2-2-6	1-11-4+	1-10-6+	2·1·1·
	BOTTOM	0-8·0+	0-6-1	0·5·1	0-5-4	0.9.1
HALF-BREADTHS	SHEER	0·0·2	1-5·1	2·1·2-	2-1-5	1-11·0
	BOTTOM	0-0·2	0-10-2	1-6-5	1-7-2	1·4·6
	KEEL PC	0-1-4	0·2·0	0·3·0	0-2-6	0-2-0

NOTES: HEIGHTS FROM BASELINE. STATIONS SPACED 3'
STEM SIDED 1½" · KEEL PC. 1" SKEG 1¼"· TRANSOM 1" (PINE)
SIDE PLANKING ½" · BOTTOM 5/8" · FRAMES SIDED 3/4",
MOULDED 1" AT TOP, 2½" AT BOTTOM · CHINE SIDED 7/8"
MOULDED 1¼" · RAIL 3/4" X 1 3/4" · SEAT RISER 5/8" X 1½" · SEATS
5/8" (PINE) · KNEES, BREAST HOOK 1" · PINE PLANK'G : ALL OTHER W.OAK

Figure 2-10.

plan rather than in or with the table of offsets. Such dimensions and information might include the distances between stations, the angle of the rudder post, the radius of a curved transom, the propeller shaft angle, aperture details, and other dimensions closely defining the outline, such as the forefoot and rudder. But designers differ in this, and rather than clutter a lines plan with detail, some will append everything possible to the offset table as a series of statements like those shown below the skiff's offsets.

Anyway, the bulk of the hull's shape (or the shape of the hull's bulk) is right there in the numbers, and you should always use every offset provided in the table due to its superiority over a paper lines plan. Paper lines plans can shrink and swell and become distorted during reproduction. I have lofted plans where one set of dimensions was consistently bigger because these dimensions had been taken off on a different day than the others. By measuring his original plan as soon as possible, the designer heads off the possibility of distortion. So, with this in mind, you should follow the old adage to "never scale a blueprint" whenever a table of offsets is available. There is only one exception to this: sometimes some offset or other given dimension is obviously so far out that you need to find out what ball park it is really in. Even the best of designers can transpose a number, put it in the wrong box, or make a mistake in rounding it off.

Preparation Work

To do the lofting, you need a work area on which you can lay down the lines of the skiff. It can be a small section of floor a little longer and taller than the boat or a piece or two of plywood arranged as a table 30 to 34 inches off the floor, since one can reach easily into the center of this boat. It only needs to be reasonably flat and smooth for drawing and able to hold the nails and picks you use to locate points, hold battens, and position the pieces you will be assembling.

"A" or "B"-grade plywood with a minimum of annoying cracks or knots makes an excellent loft surface. Its sides are reasonably true and square; it takes nails and picks well if at least ⅜″ thick and backed up, or ½″ when not; it can be picked up, transported, and stored with the lofting intact on it; it can be turned over when badly battered; and it can be used in some structure when you are through lofting on it. A coat or two of flat white paint on the lofting surface makes for good visibility and easy erasure.

The first move to make on the loft is to set up a baseline and the station lines—all as perfectly straight as possible—with the stations at right angles to the baseline. Here plywood makes life easy, for the factory edges are likely to be quite straight and true with the ends at right angles to the edges.

When you have two pieces of plywood with straight edges and square corners butted together to make a loft that is more than 12 feet long, one long edge can be the baseline for the skiff. (This will be handy for hooking on a roller tape when measuring from the base.) Then you can erect station lines that are perpendicular or "normal" to the baseline by measuring over equally, top and bottom, from an end that is square with the base.

It is an easy matter to check the edges of plywood sheets for squareness and straightness. You can check an edge for straightness by drawing a line against it and flopping the sheet over on the other side of the line. If it matches the line perfectly on the other side, the edge is straight. The squareness of an end can be checked by flopping the long edge of the sheet to either side of the line, as above, and drawing lines against the end as it is flopped on each side of the line. If the two end lines meet to form a perfectly straight line, the end is square. The sheet can also be checked for squareness of its ends by flopping it endwise along a straight line to see if the end matches its own line or adjacent angle.

If you choose to work directly on a plain floor, you can set up a baseline with a chalk line. But since it is possible to snap a curve by not lifting the line up straight and because chalk lines must be very fine to make a sharp line, it is more accurate to stretch a line taut, mark under it carefully, and connect the marks with a straightedge.

It can be handy to tack a batten on the floor for a baseline. This setup saves time and energy when measuring, as you can feel when your rule is against the baseline instead of having to look back. If you wish to set up the baseline this way, space the batten off a chalk line at each end with two of three equal width blocks, and straighten the batten by using the third as a gauge.

With the baseline established, the stations can be drawn in perpendicular to it. The stations' perpendicularity can be determined in a number of ways. Most loftsmen like to build a huge, handy-dandy square for this. Lacking one of these, you can resort to the 3-4-5 measurements that, by the Pythagorean theorem, create a right triangle. According to this theorem, when the legs measure 3 and 4 units, and the hypotenuse measures 5 of the same units, the angle formed by the legs is 90 degrees. Another method is to use the draftsman's technique. This consists of scribing two crossing arcs high above the baseline from two points equidistant on the baseline from the desired station intersection of the baseline. These arcs should cross directly above the point on the baseline where you wish to draw in the station. When these points are connected, the resulting line should be normal—you should get used to this term—to the baseline.

Speaking of arcs, the traditional tool for making long arcs in lofting is the trammel rod, which is a wood or metal bar on which two trammels with points, or a point and a pencil, can be clamped at the length of the radius wanted. Lacking this, a nail in one end of a stick and a pencil in a $5/16$-inch hole near the other end is as good, though hardly as adjustable.

You should set up the skiff's five stations just as they are in the plans, which call for stations at the extremes of bow and stern—known as perpendiculars—and three mould stations in between, all spaced 3 feet apart. The easiest way is to set up one of the stations normal to the baseline by one of the methods mentioned above, and then lay off the others with a tape or rule stretched along the base and near the top of the floor, putting in picks at the 3-foot marks.

A pick is the handiest tool in the loft. Most loftsmen use nails; there's nothing wrong with that, except that it's slower and more trouble. You can loft any boat there ever was with a few dozen ordinary ice picks, using your fist for a hammer. A pick's point is finer and harder than a nail's, and you have a handle to pull it out with. Bror Tamm, a highly regarded veteran boatbuilder, once remarked, to my delight, that only at Lawley's (where he lofted for years), Herreshoff's, and Vaitses' boatyards had he ever seen picks used in the loft. I feel lucky to have learned this method.

Anyway, we were putting in picks at the station intervals along the tape. Never mind making a pencil mark; that's an unnecessary move. Just set the pick as accurately and vertically as possible and thump it home. A straightedge slid against each pair of picks, top and bottom, gives you your station lines quickly and easily. These station lines should be promptly labeled to avoid confusion, even though there are only three of them.

With the station lines drawn, the grid is complete. You might wish to draw in the designed waterline (DWL), but on a boat this simple, and with no reference to it in the table of offsets, it is not needed as an overall reference point. However, you will need to draw in some waterlines later in order to draw stem details—but I am getting ahead of myself.

Before beginning to loft the skiff, I should explain that, as in all lofting, it will be presented in three views—profile, half-breadth, and body plan. The profile plan (also known as the elevation) shows exactly what it says, the profile of the boat. The half-

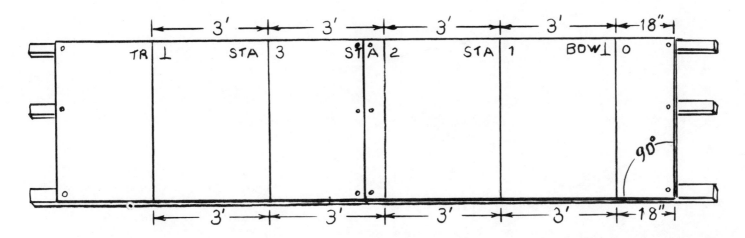

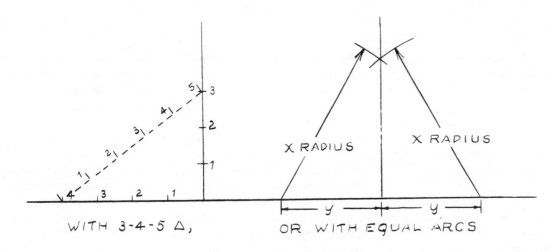

WITH 3-4-5 Δ,   OR WITH EQUAL ARCS

Above: Figure 2-11. *A lofting platform, constructed of two sheets of plywood, for the 12-foot skiff. The bottom edge serves as the baseline.*

Left: Figure 2-12. *Two methods of establishing the stations' perpendicularity: the 3-4-5 method and the draftsman's technique.*

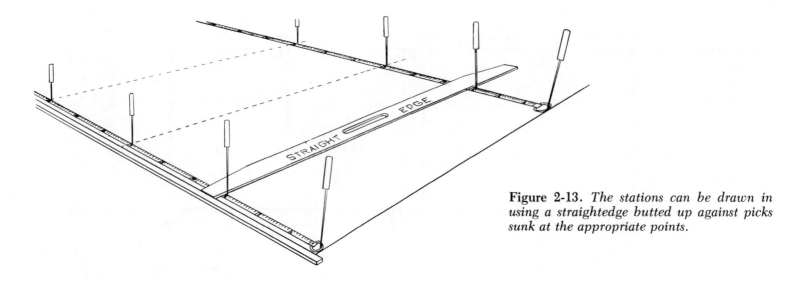

Figure 2-13. *The stations can be drawn in using a straightedge butted up against picks sunk at the appropriate points.*

breadth, or plan view, shows half of the hull split along the centerline (as seen from above or below). And as I have already discussed, the body plan shows athwartship slices of the hull as seen from both bow and stern.

At this point, there is nothing left but to start lofting the skiff. Unfortunately for those who prefer action to words, there will be more interruptions, but let's start drawing and take things as they come.

Lofting the Skiff

You should begin with the sheer, but here its ending at the transom is somewhere ahead of the aft perpendicular, so you need to fix that point first. As you can see in the lines plan, the top aft edge of the transom starts on the aft perpendicular 1″ above the height of the sheerline as given in the offsets. From there, the aft face of the transom runs as a straight line angled toward the baseline. A hypothetical extension of it would intersect the baseline at a point indicated on the plans as some given distance forward of the aft perpendicular. By placing a straightedge against picks at these points, you can draw in the transom at the proper angle. These are both cases where points are defined by dimensions given on the plans and not in the table of offsets. To mark off the points where the sheerline and the bottom meet the transom, you can either measure the heights given in the table directly up, keeping the rule normal to the baseline, or you can measure up the aft perpendicular and square over to the transom line.

Now, to draw the sheer, set picks on the stations and one on the transom at the heights above the base as given in the table. Then bend a batten around or into the curve depicted by the picks, crowding it against them with other picks as needed. It is a matter of preference whether battens are pushed into the inside of a curve or wrapped around the outside. Some loftsmen contend that it is more convenient to bend the batten in at the middle rather than to have to reach or move to both ends, where it will certainly have to be pinned if bent around. But it is also true that more picks are usually needed when the batten is bent to the inside, sometimes one at every point except the ends. Further, you often have to put in a pick past the ends anyway, as you will see.

It is best to use a relatively stiff batten for the sheer; stiffness will help guard against any extraneous humps or hollows in this long, easy curve. Obviously, stiffness in a batten is relative to the curve you ask of it, but an appropriate size in pine, fir, or spruce for this sheer might be between $\frac{3}{8}$″ x $\frac{3}{4}$″ and $\frac{1}{2}$″ x $1\frac{1}{8}$″ if bent flat, or $\frac{1}{2}$″ x $1\frac{1}{4}$″ and $\frac{5}{8}$″ x $\frac{7}{8}$″ if bent standing on edge. Not that you can't use lighter and heavier sticks; it's just that a stick is wobbly if too thin for the curve, and rebellious if too thick. The best adjusted batten, just like the best adjusted person, is one that is under neither too little nor too much stress. Therefore, it is good to have a piece of clear, even-grained stock handy to any lofting job from which you can rip different size battens as the need arises.

Now that your batten is pinned along the sheer, you should eye it critically from both ends. You are looking for two things: fairness, because you certainly don't want any kinks in this most conspicuous line, and also accuracy, which is harder to make out. To determine the sheerline's accuracy, you should study the line to see how its shape has survived magnification to full size. It should closely resemble the sheerline in the plan. Sometimes it might be a bit flat near the ends due to the ends of the batten

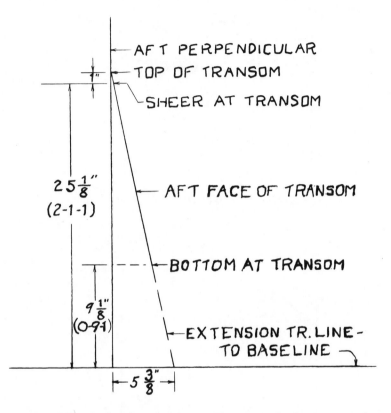

Figure 2-14. *The point where the sides meet the bottom at the transom is located by drawing in the transom at the proper angle (determined by the dimensions on the plans) and then taking the height of the lower corner of the transom from the table of offsets.*

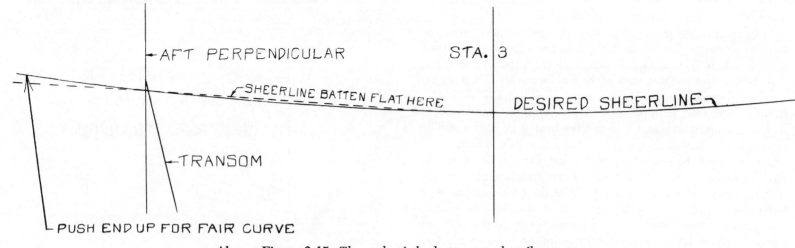

← AFT PERPENDICULAR   STA. 3

← SHEERLINE BATTEN FLAT HERE   DESIRED SHEERLINE ⌐

← TRANSOM

⌐ PUSH END UP FOR FAIR CURVE

Above: Figure 2-15. *The ends of the battens tend to flatten out over the picks and need to be pushed up.*

Below: Figure 2-16. *When a batten doesn't follow fairly the line of the picks, the loftsman must determine which point is out.*

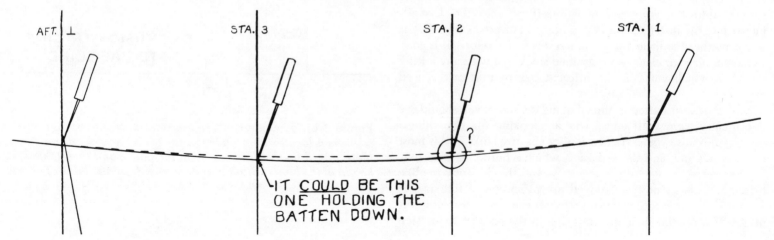

AFT. ⊥   STA. 3   STA. 2   STA. 1

?

⌐ IT COULD BE THIS
ONE HOLDING THE
BATTEN DOWN.

straightening out over the end picks, in which case you should pull up the ends of the batten gently and pin them there. This should result in a better looking line as well as one more like the plan.

Suppose one pick along the batten is badly out of line so that in no way does it seem to belong in a fair curve with the others. If you remeasure the offset, you might find that you made a mistake. If this is not the case, you should check the adjacent points; you might find that you made an error in one of these and that correcting it will bring the batten within a nudge of the point you thought was out. When all else fails to bring a bad point into line, you can assume that the designer has made a mistake. In this instance, scaling the plan may possibly "prove your point."

Regardless, you have to hold the batten to a fair line that compares most favorably with the sense of the plan and hits the most points possible. When you have accomplished this, draw the line. Before going on, you should take time to correct any mistakes that you have found in the offset table. Even if you never refer to these measurements again, you should correct them, for who wants mistakes lying around? You should also label the line you have drawn "sheer" or "top of rail."

Your next move is to draw the false stem in profile. This is a ⅝-inch-thick piece that covers the ends of the planks after they have been fastened to the stem. You will find that you need to reproduce the several lines parallel to the baseline that run aft from the bow perpendicular through the stem. These lines are called waterlines because they run through the hull parallel to the waterline. The plans indicate that they are to be spaced every 3 inches above the baseline. It is along these that you will measure the offsets that shape the curve of the stem. Place a row of picks at the measurements given on the plans between the bow perpendicular and the face of the stem and bend a thin batten around the picks. Don't forget to swing the batten's overhangs into line as

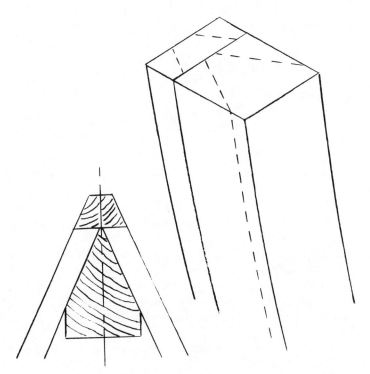

Figure 2-17. *Two views of the stem/false stem assembly.*

needed, which is more likely at the bottom with its harder curve than at the top. After sorting out any unfairness, draw in the line, carrying it 1″ below the bottom. You will want this extra wood below to cover the forward end of the keel piece.

Before moving on to draw the bottom, you can save a little time if you pause to draw in the solid line that parallels the profile of the stem in the plan. This is the aft face of the false stem. If, in

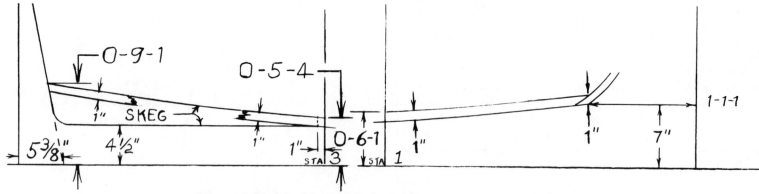

Figure 2-18. *The bottom, keel, and skeg are drawn using mea-surements from the table of offsets and the plans.*

drawing the first stem line, you bent your batten around the outside of the profile picks, you can slide a ⅝-inch block along the batten with the pencil point against it to get this line. If not, it's little trouble to measure off ⅝″ from the profile line, shifting picks as you go. This line, too, should extend to the bottom of the keel piece.

To loft the bottom, set picks at the correct heights on the stations and draw it in when the batten looks good. This closes the perimeter of the profile. While you have everything at hand, draw the bottom of the keel piece, which is 1″ thick and runs parallel to the bottom, starting at the aft face of the false stem and ending against the extension of the transom line. Also, why not put in the skeg aft, the dimensions of which are noted in the lines plan?

What you have completed is the faired profile of the skiff. Now you must draw the same lines in the plan or half-breadth view, which shows half of the boat as if you were looking at her bottom-side up. Use your baseline as a centerline and draw the view right

on top of the profile. This is not particularly confusing, since the lines are different shapes headed in different directions, and it is very handy, because any given point in one view is on the same vertical line or station in the other view. The half-breadth line of the sheer, for instance, will start on the bow perpendicular and end on the transom directly below where the profile view of it ends.

Before you draw in the half-breadth lines, you need to locate the points where the sheer and the bottom meet the transom. First, you must draw two lines normal to the base/centerline at the same horizontal point on the lofting grid as these points are located in the profile. Then, check the table of offsets for the widths of these two points and mark them off on these lines. One of these lines is the actual bottom of the transom. The other is a straight line across the transom at the sheer height. This is not the actual top of the transom, for the top extends an inch above the sheer so that, due to the transom's rake, the top aft edge is just a mite aft of this line. Because this line across the transom at the sheer does not represent the outline of the boat, you should draw it as a dashed line. We'll get to the real top of the transom later.

Having located and marked the transom edges, you can set out the picks on the stations for all of the other half-breadths of the sheer. Notice that the width of the stem face is given as 0-0-2 in the table under "half-breadth of the profile at station 0," and place a pick on the bow perpendicular ¼″ out from the centerline.

When you come to draw the half-breadth of the bottom, you will find that its starting point must be projected down to the centerline from where it meets the face of the stem in the profile view. At this foremost point, the half-breadth of the bottom is likewise ¼″.

When all is faired up, there are two more details you can put in before turning your attention from the half-breadth plan. You can draw a straight line from the bottom corner of the transom to the top corner at the sheer. This is, of course, the corner of the transom as you see it in this view. You can also draw the face of the stem, which in this plan view is a straight line ¼″ out from and parallel to the centerline, extending from the half-breadth of the sheer at station 0 to the point where it meets the bottom of the keel piece. These two details are shown in Figure 2–22.

You have now completed the outline of the skiff in two views. Because these lines have been faired so that they are "just right," you should consider these lines inviolate and use them directly in drawing the lines that are to follow.

Figure 2-19. *The sheer and bottom half-breadths at the transom are set off from the centerline at the distance out given in the table of offsets.*

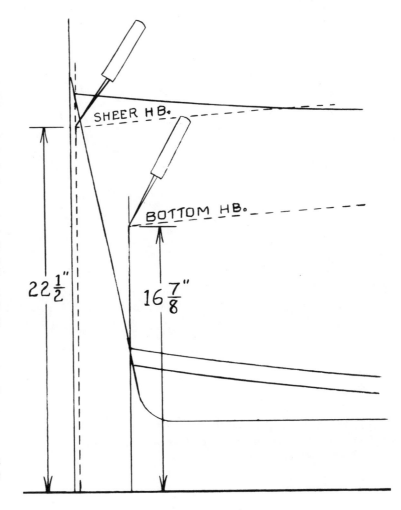

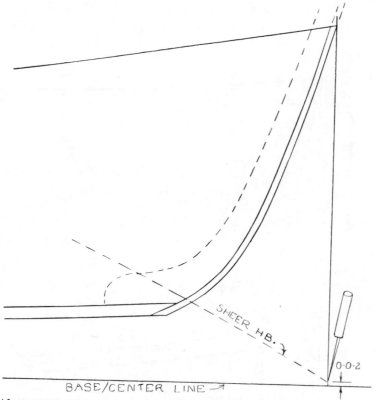

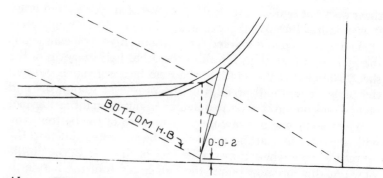

Above: Figure 2-21. *To find the forward ending of the bottom half-breadth line, project the profile ending down to the half-breadth plan and set the pick the proper distance out from the centerline.*

Above: Figure 2-20. *The sheerline in half-breadth view is started at the bow perpendicular at the distance out from the centerline given in the table of offsets.*

Right: Figure 2-22.

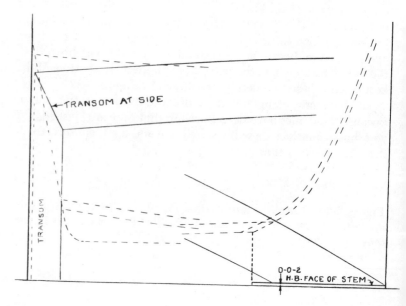

Your next move is to draw the body plan. As mentioned previously, this consists mainly of the stations in section, the transom, and a glimpse of the stem, using the midship station as a centerline. Having drawn and faired the skiff in two views and wanting the faired lines to "supersede any given measurement," many loftsmen do not go back to the table of offsets, no matter how meticulously they may have been corrected. Instead, they prefer to pick up the offsets of the lines already on the floor with pickup sticks, which are essentially long, blank, wooden rulers, and use these to lay out the next view. This is about as quick as rereading the table, and it eliminates any new mistakes in reading or measuring.

Pickup sticks can be made of straight softwood about ¼" to ⅜" thick, ½" to 1½" wide, tapered down at the edges to not over ¹⁄₁₆" thick, and carefully squared at the ends. They can easily be made on a tablesaw to any size you need, and markings are easily erased with a swipe of the hand plane or sander.

There is no standardized "system" for the usage of pickup sticks; you can assign one stick (or one side of a stick) to a line or a station, or perhaps one to heights and another to half-breadths. For drawing the skiff's sections you can pick up the four basic measurements of each station on one side of a stick. Laying the selected side of the stick along station 1 with its end against the baseline, go right up the stick ticking off (and identifying with initials) the height of the bottom, the half-breadth of the bottom, the half-breadth of the sheer, and the height of the sheer as you come to each line where it crosses the station line.

To draw the section at station 1, you must first lay the pickup stick on station 2 (which will be the centerline of the body plan) with its end against the baseline. Set a pick at the height of the bottom as marked on the pickup stick. Next, position another pick at the same height a little further to the right of the centerline than the half-breadth of the bottom. Slide a straightedge against

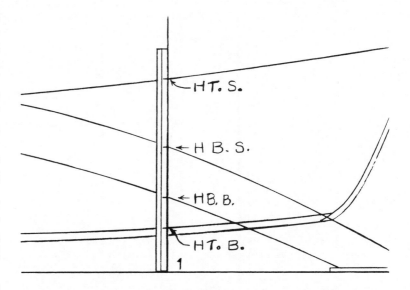

Figure 2-23. *The offsets for the body plan can be picked off each station when the profile and half-breadth drawings are complete. Above, the height at the sheer (HT. S.), the half-breadth at the sheer (HB. S.), the half-breadth at the bottom (HB. B.), and the height at the bottom (HT. B.) are picked off with a pickup stick.*

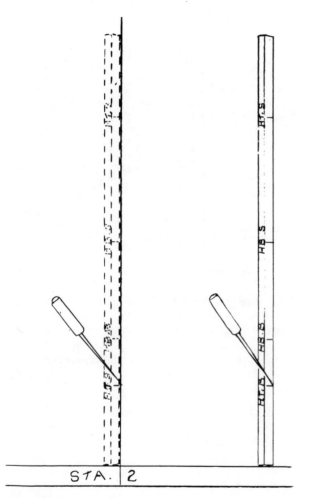

Figure 2-24. *Using a pickup stick to get the heights for the bottom of a section.*

the two picks and draw the line representing the bottom. Then set the stick along the line of the bottom and move the outboard pick to the bottom's exact half-breadth. Leave the pick right there so that later you can use it to draw the side.

Using the height of the sheer at station 1, repeat the same moves to find the outer, upper corner of this section. As this is a straight-sided boat, you can then draw the side of this section, with your straightedge against the pick at the sheer and the one that you left at the chine. With this done, the outline of the half-section is complete.

If you follow the same sequence of moves used to draw the first section, you should be able to draw the other sections with increasing rapidity, not forgetting that you should draw the after section on the left side of the centerline. With only three sections, one might be justified in drawing all three sections whole to ease the assembly of the moulds later. However, in a long boat with many similar and overlapping sections tapering toward each end, the confusion of converging lines along with the duplicated effort involved makes this practice not worth the trouble. Besides, a half-section has everything you need.

Drawing the transom comes next; in the body plan this should be done in the same manner as the rest of the sections. When you finish drawing its half-section, it should look just like the three sections already in place. In reality, it isn't; it shows the correct width and height in a *visual* sense as seen from directly aft, but it does not show the true top-to-bottom length or shape of the surface of the transom. This is because, unlike the other sections, which are vertical slices, the transom is raked. So if you built a transom for this skiff from the body plan view, it would be too short to fit the boat—but more about that later. (This does not apply to vessels with plumb transoms.)

With the transom section in place in the body plan, the skiff should now look like Figure 2–25 on the loft floor. It seems to be a

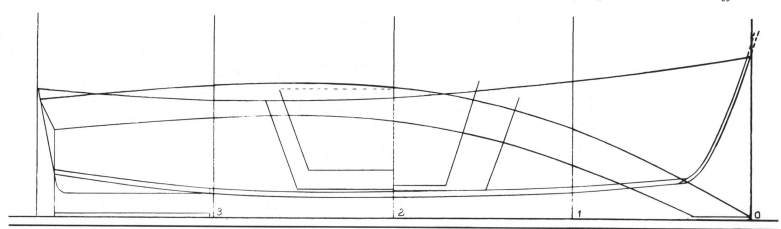

Figure 2-25.

rather naked set of bones, so why not fill in some of the missing pieces? First, a top on the transom half-section, which is a line from the sheer to the centerline. The designer shows a fair sweep rising from the sheer to 1″ higher than the sheer in the center. This is probably because the transoms of open boats don't look right if flat on top and flush with the sheer. While such a transom top will work out on a rowing model, it won't if an outboard of any size is to live on the transom. In this case the transom top should be straight, with a notch to accommodate a certain shaft length. This configuration, too, can be made to look better if the whole thing is raised up an inch and the ends rounded down to the sheer in an ogee curve. Very often when the designer isn't around, or if the designer has shown alternative details in the plans, the loftsman will have to make changes like this to suit the owner's requirements.

If the top of the transom is to be a curve, the important thing to remember in drawing it in the half-section is that it should not be rising when it meets the centerline, because when the two sides are joined, they will meet in a point. To avoid this, the curve is best drawn full length against a straight line by bending a batten over at least three points between the ends. Sometimes the designer will give offsets for a curve he wants, or you could use one of the methods of drawing deck beam crowns discussed later in the book. Or, what the heck, just push the batten out with three picks that divide the line's length into four parts until you like its curve.

When the curve is drawn, set up the offsets for half of it off a sheer-level line on the transom in the body plan and draw it in.

You should now consider this transom top in the other views, because, properly, any line shown in one view should appear in

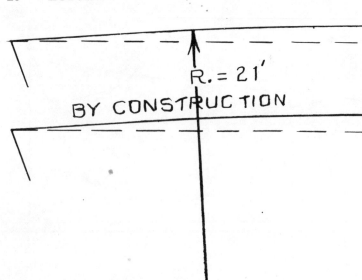

WITH RADIUS

R. = 21'

BY CONSTRUCTION

Figure 2-26. *Two methods of drawing crowns. With the radius method, an arc is swung using a radius of a length specified by the designer. In constructing a crown, a known height of crown is divided proportionately and applied at equal intervals along a known crown length.*

the others, though in some views it may take a form that doesn't seem to amount to much. In the profile, the curved transom top already exists as the just-over-1-inch extension of the transom line that we drew from sheer to aft perpendicular (from the side we see only its height and rake).

Turning to the half-breadth view, it is clear that the top of the transom will be a shallow curve from the sheer to the centerline due to the rake of the transom. But precisely what path, what curve in the fore-and-aft direction through this narrow space in the half-breadth view does the top edge take? Well, you can establish any point of this line if you refer to the body plan and the profile.

Say you want to pinpoint the line's location (fore-and-aft location is what we are looking for) at a certain distance out from the centerline. I will call it point A despite the fact that it is not yet a point but an athwartship distance at which you wish to fix a point. Point A will have a certain vertical dimension above the sheerline/transom juncture that you can easily determine in the body plan by taking a measurement at its distance out from the centerline. Then take the height of point A from the body plan to

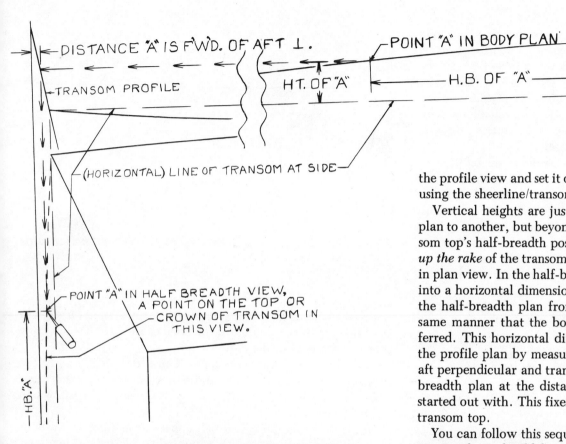

DISTANCE "A" IS FWD. OF AFT ⊥.

POINT "A" IN BODY PLAN

TRANSOM PROFILE

HT. OF "A"

H.B. OF "A"

(HORIZONTAL) LINE OF TRANSOM AT SIDE

POINT "A" IN HALF BREADTH VIEW,
A POINT ON THE TOP OR
CROWN OF TRANSOM IN
THIS VIEW.

H.B. "A"

Figure 2-27. *The fore-and-aft location of any point (A) on the crown of the raked transom is found by projection—from body plan, to profile, to half-breadth view.*

the profile view and set it off vertically on the line of the transom, using the sheerline/transom juncture height as a base.

Vertical heights are just fine for transferring points from one plan to another, but beyond that, they can't help you fix the transom top's half-breadth position any further. It's point A's height *up the rake* of the transom that gives you its fore-and-aft location in plan view. In the half-breadth view, this height is transformed into a horizontal dimension that can be projected downwards to the half-breadth plan from point A in the profile in much the same manner that the bottom terminus of the stem was transferred. This horizontal dimension can also be determined from the profile plan by measuring point A's distance forward of the aft perpendicular and transferring this measurement to the half-breadth plan at the distance out from the centerline that you started out with. This fixes point A as a point of the curve of the transom top.

You can follow this sequence to fix any number of points, but two or three should be plenty to pin down this feeble curve. Though I admit this line doesn't affect the building of a beautiful skiff, it is important as a case in finding your way around, and of being able to forge a missing link in one view with information brought from other views. One hears a lot about how hard it is to loft transoms, but unless you consider the above moves difficult, that's the wrong word. Time consuming, even tedious, yes, but the only thing that might be difficult is *recalling or researching what information to get in which views and in what sequence.*

While working in this area, you can put a little flesh on the transom in profile by drawing its top and forward faces. The thickness of the transom having been given as 1″, draw a line parallel to the aft face 1″ forward of it. This line should be solid above the sheer and dashed or dotted below if you carry it inside the boat to the bottom, which is optional.*

To finish the transom in profile, cap the top of the bit of transom peeping above the sheer with a line parallel to the sheer.

From the transom, you should turn to completing the drawing of the stem and keel piece. Both of these would have been more developed before being drawn in the body plan in a hull whose sections faired into them, but here station 1 is aft of the stem and the keel is external to the skiff's flat bottom. The keel has been drawn in profile but is missing from the body and half-breadth plans. Draw its half-breadth first because it has shape in that view, and if it needs fairing there, you can then use the corrected offsets in drawing it in the body plan. To start, set your picks at the half-breadths given in the table of offsets for the transom and stations. Setting the pick at the bow is not quite as easy, however, as the width given in the table of offsets for the keel at the bow is wider than the aft face of the false stem into which the keel runs. You must put the forward pick at that point on the half-breadth

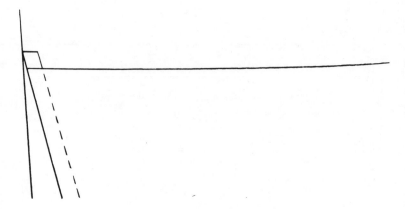

Figure 2-28. *The transom is finished in profile by drawing in its top and forward faces.*

line of the bottom that is the same width as the dimension given in the table; from there forward the edge of the keel has the same shape as the edge of the bottom.

Also, as part of the keel's half-breadth drawing, project the skeg's forward ending in the profile down to the centerline, and draw its half-breadth from there to the transom as shown in Figure 2–29.

In the body plan, the keel will appear as rectangular sections with slightly varying widths and heights. These dimensions should be gotten with pickup sticks from the other two views at the stations. One thing that you should note when picking up these dimensions is that the keel depth in these sections is the same as the 1-inch thickness of the keel piece only near station 2, where the keel lies perpendicular to the station line. Elsewhere, it is a mite deeper due to the sweep of the bottom. We will encounter

---

*In a lines plan, all of the lines represent the outside of the boat, unless otherwise labeled or drawn as dashed or dotted lines. Sometimes lines plans have been drawn to the inside of the planking, plating, etc., so that the framing can be picked up without deducting the thickness of the skin, but these are the exceptions, which the designer should note on the plan or the offsets. Some designers also mention that the lines are to the outside, though this should be understood when not contradicted.

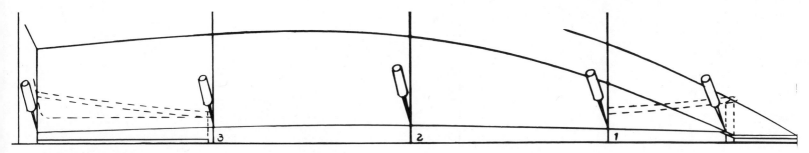

Figure 2-29.

this circumstance again when we take up deducting planking thickness to arrive at exact frame and bulkhead dimensions and shapes.

Before leaving the body plan, you should draw the skeg, which (as shown in the construction plan) is notched through the keel and fits against the bottom planking. While you are at it, you should show this notch in the profile by putting a dotted line up through the keel at the forward end of the skeg.

Now to complete the stem. A portion that is clearly missing in the lofting thus far is its aft face in profile. This should be shown as a dotted line with a "paw" at the bottom. The designer has provided its "molded" dimensions (its fore-and-aft measurements as opposed to its athwartship width, or "sided" dimension) on the plan. Using these dimensions, set off a row of picks, bend in a batten from well above the sheer to as far down as the beginning of the paw, and draw this much of the aft face. To get the sharp curve of the paw, you will need a very limber batten (such as a piece of bandsaw blade) or a compass, or perhaps even a coffee can. All's fair in drawing the many tight curves like this found in boat construction. Often, because the exact curve is not important, the designer doesn't bother to give offsets or radii, nor do

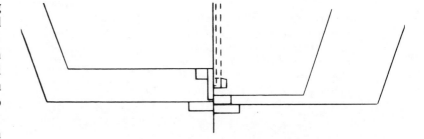

Figure 2-30. *The keel appears in the body plan as rectangular sections.*

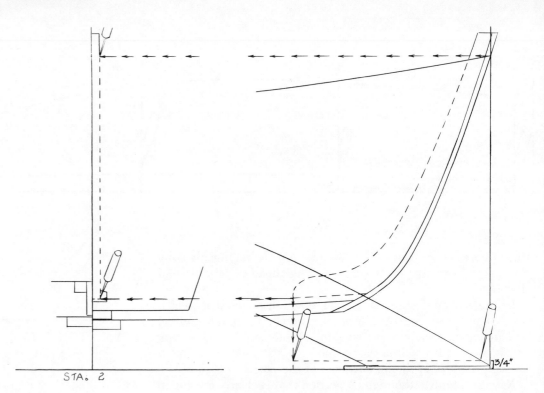

Figure 2-31. *After the stem is drawn in profile, its endings are projected to the half-breadth and plan views, and then it is drawn in in those views parallel to the centerline.*

STA. 2

you need to get fussy about it. Just think about practicalities and a fair shape; if it looks right, it usually is.

Before you can complete the foot of the stem, you have to draw in a short piece of the bottom planking on which the paw rests. From the scantlings included with the table of offsets, you know it is ⅝″ thick, and to avoid confusion with the skiff's lines, you should draw it as a dashed line, or use a different color. If you feel artistic, you could even shade it with lines like the end grain of wood.

To show the stem in the half-breadth view, you first need to project the aft end of the foot down to the centerline. Then draw a dotted line parallel to the centerline ¾″ away (one-half of the

stem's 1½″ sided dimension), from the aft end of the foot to where it intersects the half-breadth of the sheer. To draw it in the body plan, transfer its lowest height from the profile, draw a dotted line from there parallel to the centerline ¾″ away (extending it well above the sheer), and then square off the bottom over to the centerline.

You will also want to show the forward face of the stem. This is, of course, on the same line in the profile as the aft face of the false stem, but you do not know the half-breadths of this face. What you do know is that it is already drawn ⅝″ behind the face of the false stem in the profile; that by projecting its intersection with the sheer and bottom lines in the profile down to the

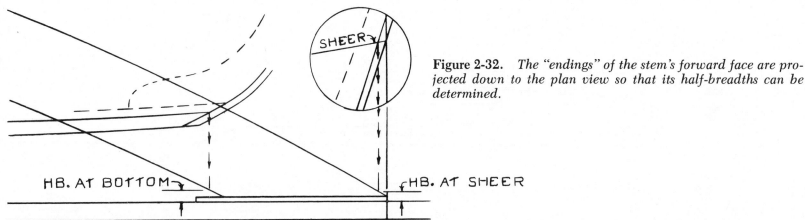

Figure 2-32. *The "endings" of the stem's forward face are projected down to the plan view so that its half-breadths can be determined.*

centerline you can find where they cross the half-breadths of sheer and bottom; and that these crossings will give you its half-breadths at sheer and bottom.

If you look at the plans closely, you will note that, in reality, the stem doesn't intersect the bottom. How, then, can you get away with applying a measurement to the stem at this point when it hasn't really been measured there at all? The answer is that this is simply a shortcut. To get the half-breadth at or near the stem's bottom terminus, you would need to draw in another waterline slightly above where the bottom half-breadth line intersects the stem. By extending the stem the slight distance necessary to make it intersect the bottom, you don't have to draw in this extra waterline. Since this difference in distance is minor, and since there is relatively little taper to the stem, it doesn't matter if you simply use what is there.

You now know the width of the stem face at the sheer and you have a close approximation of its width at its lower end. If this were a straight-stemmed, straight-sectioned boat, this would be all that you would need; you could connect the determined widths with a straight line. However, this is not the case here, for the stem is curved. Instead of maintaining straight sections through to the bow, the curved stem introduces a slight "cheek" or "pouch" in the sections near the bow. This means that the stem will flare outward toward the bottom, due to the different angles at which the sides close with the stem from top to bottom. You must therefore have some reference points in between to map out the stem's changing cross-sections.

Reference points can be established on the stem/false stem line by drawing in intermediate waterlines. Draw a waterline at some point between the sheer and bottom running through the profile and body plans. Then pick up its half-breadths in the body plan, set these off from the centerline at the stations in plan view, and draw the waterline's half-breadth configuration in the same manner that the sheer and bottom were drawn in this view. Draw in at least one other waterline on the topsides to be sure that you have enough information to accurately draw the stem shape.

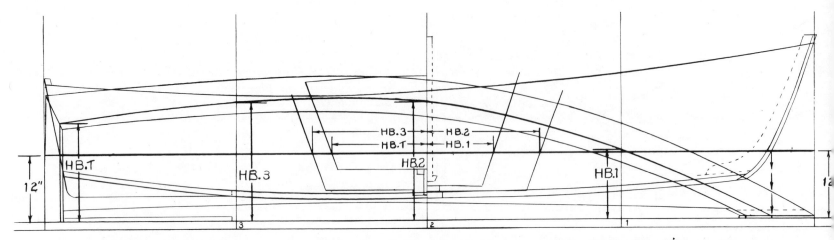

Figure 2-33. *The loftsman need not refer only to the lines that the designer provides; he can draw in lines wherever he needs additional reference points. Here, an extra waterline has been drawn in to gain an additional point to help determine the line of the stem's forward face.*

These waterlines should fall into place very nicely if the sheer and bottom are fair, because when the latter are connected by straight sides, it is axiomatic that the entire surface between them will reflect their shapes. You may find that the extra reference points provided by these additional waterlines will be useful elsewhere.

Anyway, with the waterlines drawn, you can now sweep in the half-breadth of the stem/false stem line, which is what started this business. You can also take it into the body plan and draw it there, as shown in Figure 2–34. The stem will have the same half-breadths at the waterlines in this view as it has at the waterlines in the half-breadth view. You should carry it, along with the face of the false stem (which is but a line parallel to the centerline ¼" away), from well above the sheer down to the lowest point of each in the profile, where you should square each off to the centerline. Both of these are solid lines, being on the outside of the boat.

At this point, about the only unfinished part of the lofting is the absence of the sheerline in the body plan. This you can now neatly draw, starting from its intersection with the face of the stem (which you should project over from the profile) and sloping down and around through the sheer height-at-side of each station. The line twists away over station 2 and reappears at station 3 on the other side, and to draw it neatly, you had best put the sheer point of station 3 on the right-hand side and the point of station 2 on the left. Then you can easily draw the short bend in the sheer that is close to the last station on each side. (*See* Figure 2–35.)

It is optional whether you draw the chine (corner of bottom and side) in this view, or whether you draw the two lines that

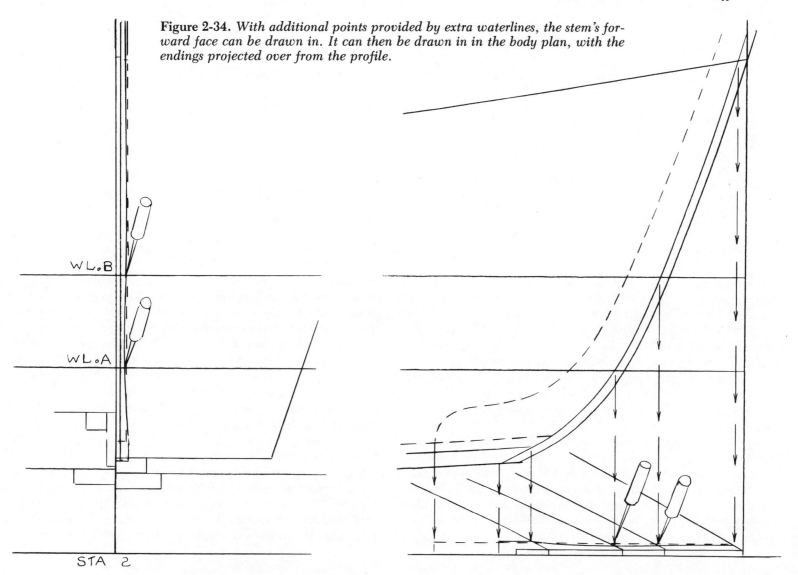

Figure 2-34. *With additional points provided by extra waterlines, the stem's forward face can be drawn in. It can then be drawn in in the body plan, with the endings projected over from the profile.*

WL.B

WL.A

STA 2

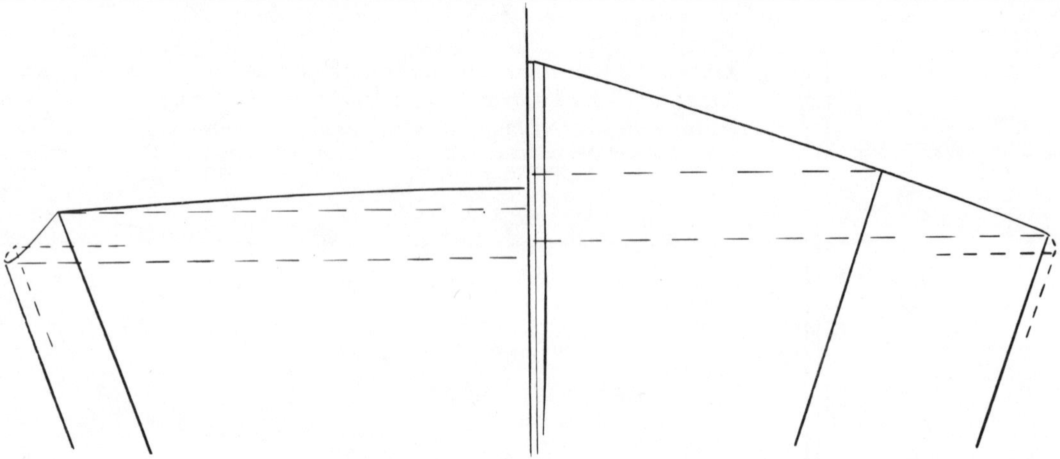

Figure 2-35. *To get the proper curve in the body plan sheerline, it is helpful to draw in an adjacent station on each side.*

define the upper and lower outboard edges of the keel. As you have seen with the sheer, there are not enough stations to establish these lines very reliably. The only reason you might be glad to have the chines drawn in would be if you wanted to make some deck chocks or perhaps a shipping cradle that fitted around the hull between stations. For such a loose, padded fit, the chines would help you pick up the shape more quickly. Otherwise, the lines would be just for looks and to tie things together. But here (in Figure 2–36) the body plan is shown with the three lines drawn in.

At this point in the lofting, everything "given" by the designer has been laid down. From here on, it is all downhill, since you only need a little more drawing here and there to be able to pick up the parts and set them up. Unfortunately, for those of you who may be impatient, I must add the usual whys and wherefores for those remaining parts, but if you would prefer to "read the pictures" only, more power to you.

Thus far in the lofting, there has been no view of the transom showing its true size and shape, so you'll have to make a separate drawing of its half-section to get a pattern that will work. Since the profile has the transom's true heights along its raked aft face, the easiest way to draw it to its true dimensions is to project the pattern square off the transom line in the profile, using the profile as the centerline. Whether you project to the left or right is optional; to the left is more clear of conflicting lines, but as there often isn't enough floor space to do it in this manner, you are more likely to find yourselves working to the right. Though one soon gets used to overlapping views, it does help to use a different-color pencil.

Use a big square and project the lines of bottom and sheer out from their intersections with the transom line (the bottom as a solid line, the sheer as a dashed line), mark their half-breadths with picks, and then draw the side of the transom between them. You must then concern yourself with drawing precisely the same

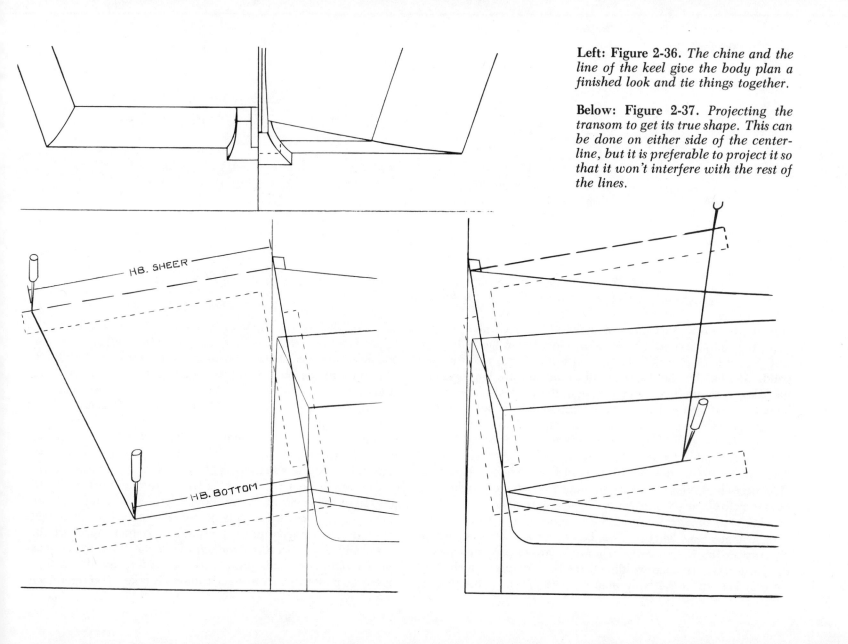

Left: Figure 2-36. *The chine and the line of the keel give the body plan a finished look and tie things together.*

Below: Figure 2-37. *Projecting the transom to get its true shape. This can be done on either side of the centerline, but it is preferable to project it so that it won't interfere with the rest of the lines.*

H.B. SHEER

H.B. BOTTOM

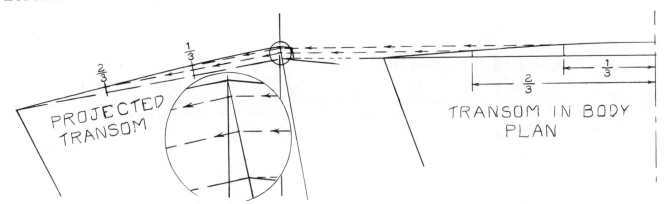

Figure 2-38. *The heights of the transom crown must be passed through the raked transom in profile to get the correct crown in the body plan.*

curved top on this pattern that is shown in the body plan, which requires you to carry the heights of the curve from the body plan to the profile, and finally to the pattern. This procedure "expands" the heights the slight amount that they are longer along the raked transom line than they are in the vertical plane of the body plan. If you did not follow this procedure but took the heights directly from body plan to expanded half pattern, the resulting curve would be flatter than that which is called for. In this boat it wouldn't make a bit of difference, but if there were a deck, the top of the transom wouldn't fit worth a hoot. Regardless of its necessity in this instance, you might as well learn right now how to get the curve or crown to come out as given.

When you drew the top of the transom in the half-breadth plan, you got some heights in the body plan and set them off on the transom line in the profile. These can now be projected out on the pattern to the same widths off the centerline at which they were picked up in the body plan to help you draw the proper

curve of the top in the half-breadth view. If, however, you skipped drawing the top of the transom in the half-breadth plan, you must now come to terms with the curve. Measure off from the centerline in the body plan two points that roughly divide the transom top into three parts, take the heights of these points to the profile, and mark them on the aft face of the transom. Then square these points over the same distances from the centerline on the half-pattern as on the body plan. This establishes two correct points in the curve of the top of the pattern to go with the centerline and sheer heights, which are already in place.

You now have a true drawing from which to pick up a half-pattern of the transom. At this point, you should remember that this is the *aft* face of the transom, that all boats (except straight-sided, square-ended punts) get smaller as they approach the stern, and that, therefore, *the outside of the transom is always smaller than the inside on at least two sides* (usually on three sides), no matter which way the transom is raked. Therefore, you

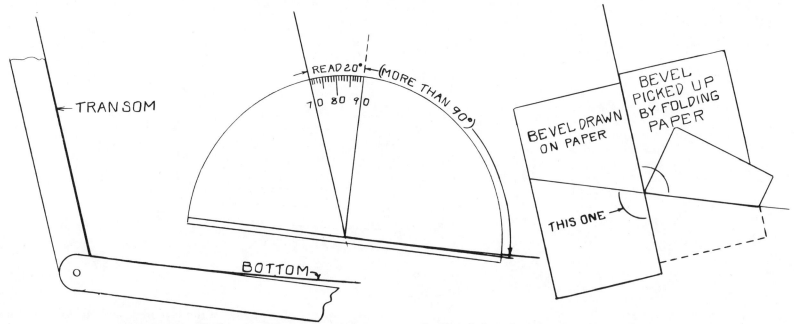

Figure 2-39. *The bevel of the transom's bottom can be lifted directly from the plans. Three methods are shown above.*

need to know how much bigger it should be at these inside faces so that it won't be too small to fit against the skin there.

It will be no trouble getting this information as far as the angle of bottom to transom is concerned. It's right there in the profile, and you can pick it up by reading it with a protractor, by reproducing the actual angle with a bevel square or a folded piece of paper, or by tracing it on a piece of paper.

When you read the degrees, take only those between the 90-degree line on the protractor and the line being measured (*see* Figure 2–40); what you want to know is how many degrees more or less than square to bevel the part. If you are working with a tablesaw, this also tells you how many degrees to tilt the saw or the saw table, which are already at 90 degrees to one another.

Standard practice is to mark the number of degrees as either "X-degrees S" ("S" for standing) or "X-degrees U" ("U" for under), depending on whether the bevel stands out from the side you are marking from or cuts under from there. (That is to say, use "S" when the overall angle is obtuse and "U" when the overall angle is acute.) So to indicate the kind of bevel required for the bottom of the skiff's transom you should mark it on the pattern as "X-degrees S."

If you have lifted the actual aft-face-to-bottom angle, you can simply draw that angle on the pattern near the edge to which it applies and draw an arc from leg to leg within that angle to identify it as such. Then, when you come to cutting the edge of the transom, you can set your bevel square at the angle drawn on the

Right: Figure 2-41. *A transom side bevel picked up from
the half-breadth plan can be
properly marked out on the
stock if the bevel for the top is
cut first and the side bevels
then applied in that plane.*

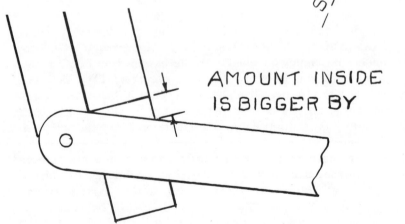

AFT FACE
OF TRANSOM

SIDE

TOP

BEVEL FIRST

SHEER

Figure 2-40. *A bevel can be stated
as the difference in length between
the two faces of a member.*

AMOUNT INSIDE
IS BIGGER BY

pattern and place it against the saw blade and table while tilting
same. To check the finished cut, you have only to compare it to
the angle you have picked up with your bevel square.

A different approach to stating the bevel on the lofting or pattern is to state the amount larger that the inside is than the outside. This amount is the difference between a squared edge and
the beveled edge, and can be found easily by squaring off the bottom of the transom in profile and measuring the spread between
the beveled and squared lines on the forward face. Write this difference on the pattern, followed by a " + " or "−" for bigger or
smaller. (*See* Figure 2-40.)

You can establish the bevel on the sides of the transom in much
the same way you did on the bottom by taking the angles of side
to transom at sheer and bottom as they have been drawn in the
half-breadth plan. But be careful! The angle you see as you look
down on the intersection of the sheer or the bottom with the tran-

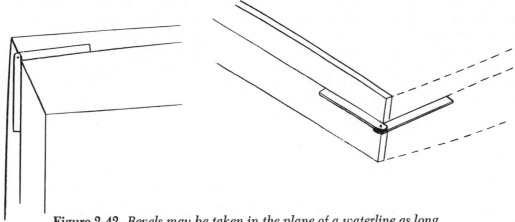

Figure 2-42. *Bevels may be taken in the plane of a waterline as long as the bevel is marked out in that plane.*

som is not an angle taken normal to the aft face of the transom (as it was when you took the angle of the bottom in the profile view) but is an angle taken in a tilted plane, due to the rake of the transom, the flare of the sides, and the upward sweep of sheer and bottom, not to mention the curve in the top of the transom. This angle is a more horizontal one than the one you would get if you held a bevel square flat on the two surfaces of the boat, and normal to the corner. To get an accurate bevel, then, you must hold the bevel square *in the same plane represented in the plan* with, for instance, one leg along the transom's top edge and the other headed along the rail.

The easiest way to ensure that the bevel square is being held in the correct plane is to make the angle cuts on the top and bottom of the transom first and then mark in the bevel. After the proper bevel has been cut on the top and bottom, place the bevel square with its blade lying flat on one of these angled edges and with the

body lying along its edge. You now know that your bevel square is in the correct plane for marking the bevel. After being marked, the bevels can be sawn. Tilt the saw blade (or the saw table) to match the bevel and angle the transom stock so that the saw blade is in line with the line of the cut (which has been drawn on the surface of the stock).

A better way to get the correct bevel of the transom's sides is to work from the angles of waterlines in the half-breadth plan. Even though these waterlines are not normal to the raked transom, they are much more so than the sheer or bottom in this boat and would be exactly so if the transom were plumb. So here, you are picking up an angle that will only be accurate for making bevels when the bevel square is held in the plane of the waterline. You can provide that plane by marking the waterline across the aft face and edge of the transom, and holding the bevel square against these lines when marking the bevels. Another way is to make a little wedge that reproduces the angle between the transom and the stations, which, when slipped small end up between the body of the bevel square and the transom, aligns the bevel square in the plane of the waterline.

All you need to remember about transom bevels, then, are these two points: You should try to make them in those angles that are most normal to the surface of the transom; and second, any angle taken in a plane not normal to the surface is only valid for marking bevels when it is returned to that plane. It is ignorance and disregard of these points that make so many transoms fit almost right, but not quite.

At this point, the "laying down" part of the skiff's lofting is relatively complete: the lines are drawn and faired full size, and the stem, three stations, and the transom are amply defined. The next move is to "pick up" these five items and "set them up."

Whether or not he is going to set up and build the boat, the lofts-man must know the method of construction to be used. From the start of lofting he must be thinking about which stations will be used to make moulds, which might be used for frames or bulkheads, and what sort of profile pieces, patterns, or forms will have to be made. He also has to know whether the hull will be built upright or upside down, for it is his job to provide markings to facilitate leveling up an upright hull, and to provide for some sort of extension of the parts of an upside-down hull to hold them at the correct height off the floor or strongback.

Many small boats are built upright rather than upside down. It is easier to build lapstrake hulls this way, as one has only to reach down inside to clench the laps. Boats with fore-and-aft or plywood-planked bottoms are also often built upright, with the bottom gotten out first and topped off with chines, cleats, floors, and frames for planking. If this is the way you wish to proceed with the 12-foot skiff, go ahead and make up the five essential parts that will be attached to the bottom. A common setup for upright building would look like that shown in Figure 3–1.

On the other hand, if you are going to have a cross-planked bottom or use fiberglass or glued-and-nailed-strip construction, you would probably choose an upside-down setup. I say "prob-ably" because with ingenuity and planning most building methods can be managed either right side up or upside down—every time you turn around some bright chap has come

up with a new way to get a hull together. Strip-built and one-off fiberglass boats can also be built upright on the inside of temporary moulds.

If the boat is to be built bottom up, you should make provisions for each part to reach the floor while picking it up in the loft. To accomplish this, you need only draw a reference line across the top of your lofting to which to extend the components of the frames. Called the "floor line" or the "top of the floor line," its height, aside from clearing the highest point of the sheer, is a matter of convenient working height. With small boats there is room for argument about what is the best height, but as size increases, it is more a matter of how low you can set the stem or highest part and still manage with it. Anyway, since all of the parts of the skiff are drawn level and true to the base of the lofting, they will set up at the proper heights when extended to any floor line that is parallel to the baseline. Some of the usual types of extension for upside-down moulds are shown in Figure 3–2.

You are now almost ready to pick up the skiff, but first you need to make the planking deductions from the lines to get the shapes and dimensions of the moulds. Remember that most lofting is done to the *outside* of the planking and that when this is the case and you are building the hull over moulds, bulkheads, frames, or a rack, you must reduce the size of these parts by the thickness of the planking or skin in order to keep that skin within the lines. Further, in the case of temporary racks for one-off

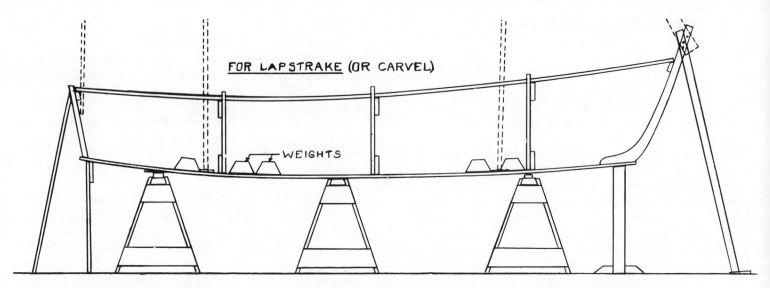

FOR LAPSTRAKE (OR CARVEL)

WEIGHTS

Above: Figure 3-1. *The setup for the upright construction of small carvel and lapstrake hulls.* **Below: Figure 3-2.** *Typical extensions to the floor in moulds used in upside-down setups.*

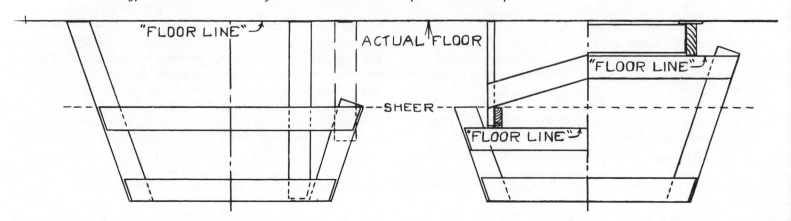

"FLOOR LINE"

ACTUAL FLOOR

"FLOOR LINE"

SHEER

"FLOOR LINE"

"FLOOR LINE"

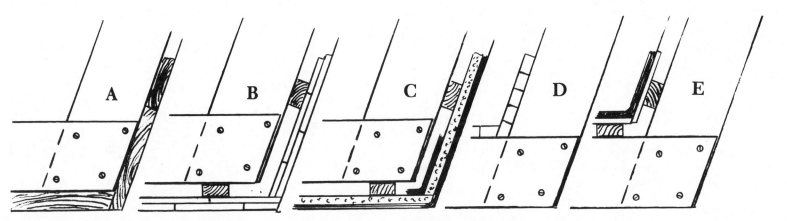

Figure 3-3. *The nature of the deductions varies with each construction type. For wooden construction over moulds (A), you need deduct the planking only. With a laminated skin built up over moulds and stringers (B), the stringer thickness as well as the skin thickness needs to be deducted. In foam-cored fiberglass construction (C), deductions are made for the ribbands, the foam core, and the fiberglass skin. For strip planking on the inside of moulds (D), there is no deduction needed. Where a fiberglass hull is molded on the inside of a female mold (E), the thickness of the ribbands and the liner must be added on to the moulds.*

fiberglass construction and longitudinally framed cold-molded wooden boats where the ribbands or stringers may be fastened on the outside of moulds, the moulds will have to be smaller by the thickness of the planking plus the thickness of the stringers or ribbands.

If you are thinking of building the hull *inside* any sort of rack or mold (meaning a mold or cavity for plastic construction) where the moulds would be part of a framework around the *outside* of the boat, you must take the opposite tack. You will have to add on to the lines the thickness of whatever lining and/or stringers that might come between the outside of the hull and the moulds you are picking up. Also, in this kind of setup, the transom and stem-forming frameworks will have to be pushed to the outside of the boat, allowing for the thickness of any material lining them.

All of this is not as complicated as my trying to put it into words has made it sound. You will never have any trouble with it if you follow these simple steps: start with the hull line, which is the outside of the skin, draw the skin at its proper thickness inside that line (if deducting), draw any structural members that will be between the mould and the skin at their thicknesses, and so on,

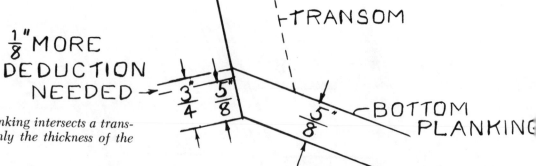

Figure 3-4. *Strictly speaking, if the planking intersects a transverse member at an angle, deducting only the thickness of the planking stock will be insufficient.*

until you come to your mould. That's where it's at, and that's how to deduct or add on to the lines before picking them up as moulds.

Your deductions or add-ons are obviously drawn parallel to the lines in the body plan. Since the 12-foot skiff's section lines are straight, you should be able to do this rapidly, using an offset at each end and a straightedge. To avoid confusion and the very real possibility of mistakenly picking up the wrong line, you should draw these mould lines in a different color, or as dashed lines, or both.

Note that the skiff's transom half-pattern also must be reduced by the thickness of the planking at both the bottom and sides. Strictly speaking, if you deduct only the planking widths—⅝″ for the bottom and ½″ for the sides—your deductions won't be large enough; you will need to deduct a bit more, due to the angles at which the planking and transom meet. To find the precise amount of the deduction, you can draw two parallel lines spaced the thickness of the planking in question and mark an angle across them as if it were the transom intercepting the planking; the

length of the crossing line would be the amount you should deduct.

Now, I just know that along about here a light will go on in some bright brain, and the chap will ask, "Well, if the thickness of the planking passing at an angle calls for a bigger deduction from the transom, wouldn't it also call for different amounts of deduction on all of the moulds except perhaps the midship mould, which is the only one that the planking meets squarely?"

Theoretically, he is absolutely right, but in practice, to make the hundreds of slight adjustments as the angle changes from station to station (and up and down each station) just wouldn't be worth it in this case. In most instances you would be dealing with very small errors that change too gradually to affect fairness at all. Only in boatbuilding projects with deep stringers, thick planking, foam core, or those with very bluff bows or sterns—all of which call for large deductions—would the differences even be worth mentioning.

If you are one who takes pleasure in making startling statements, then you could make this statement: "No hull whose body plan was deducted from or added to in making moulds is exactly as designed. It is actually a tiny bit bigger (or a tiny bit smaller) at both ends." To keep your perspective in such matters you should remember that every design is the result of some designer's rather instinctive, arbitrary, subjective decision-making, and that as he drew it, he may well have been torn between bigger differences than any conscientious loftsman might come up with. So it's more important to be concerned with fairness and with accuracy in maintaining that fairness in whatever you pick up, set up, and build.

I apologize to those who have not found this digression interesting, but you can bet that there is some egghead somewhere, his sealed beams aglow with mathematical joy, working on a computer program to compensate for what I term the "DAE" (Deduction Angle Error). What it all amounts to is that here you shouldn't be really uptight about whether to deduct the straight $\frac{5}{8}$" and $\frac{1}{2}$", or measure the amounts at the angles of the transom, or whether somebody with a computer claims he can loft a boat that is within $\frac{1}{100}$" (just ask him if he can build her within that tolerance and why he needs to). You just want to build your boat nice and neat, that's all.

You have to deduct for the planking or skin on the stem also. In traditional wooden boats, this deduction has always been in the form of the cut-out rabbet. In this skiff, however, the rabbet is formed partly by a bevel on the main stem and partly by the aft face of the false stem, which will cover the hood ends of the planks. To find the ready-to-plank shape of the stem proper, you must make planking deductions from its cross-sections. These are already partly drawn in the half-breadth plan, which shows the half-breadths at the sheer, at two waterlines, and at the bottom, and a line representing the half-siding of the stem that runs from the forward perpendicular to the stem's aft extremity. All you need to complete each section is the aft face of the stem, projected

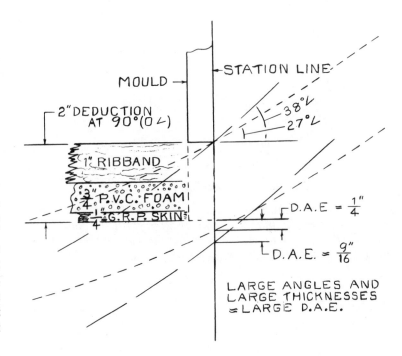

Figure 3-5.

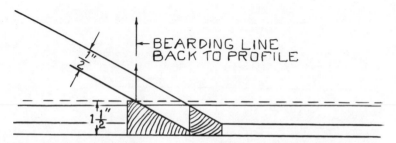

Figure 3-6. *The deduction at the stem is made perpendicular to the planking so the planking will lie flush with the false stem. With the deduction made, the bearding line can be taken back to the profile for transfer to the pattern.*

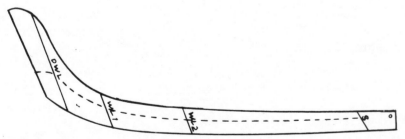

Figure 3-7. *The stem pattern with the bearding line pattern marked on it.*

down from profile to half-breadth view. You can then make your deduction from each section by drawing a short line to represent the planking parallel to the half-breadth line, ½" inside of it, from the aft face of the false stem to wherever the line crosses the half-siding of the main stem. Here is a case where you *should* make the effort to deduct normal to the half-breadth line, for you want to bring the half-breadth in to meet a predetermined width, i.e., the outside face of the false stem, whose width was established in the half-breadth plan earlier. If instead, the deduction is measured normal to the centerline, the rabbet would be too shallow and the false stem wouldn't quite cover the hood ends of the planking. When the lines are drawn, you might dress up each stem section with some identifying artwork.

Now that you have some sectional shapes for the stem (and the false stem, too), you know what shaping will be required after the stem has been cut out of 1½" stock to the stem pattern that you will pick up from the profile. But before you pick up that pattern—there's always one more "before you . . ." in this lofting business—you can pick up the offsets of the bearding line (the line of the aftermost edge of the rabbet on the stem) from the half-sections, and draw it in the profile to be picked up on the pattern and transferred to the stem. (*See* Figure 3–6.)

If you are going to build a number of boats, and therefore a number of stems, you can also make a half-pattern of the face of the main stem, drawn with the offsets of its half-breadths in the sections. Admittedly, this is too roundabout for building one stem, since it requires a separate drawing, which might as well be made on the stem itself after it has been cut to profile. This line, the line of the forward inside edge of the planking, which wavers very slightly according to the changing angle of the planking with the stem (same as the bearding line does), is called the back rabbet line. It would be the deepest part or back corner of the rabbet in the side of a solid stem. The only view in the lofting that shows the stem face/back rabbet line full length is the profile; in the other two views it is foreshortened. So to make a pattern of it, you would have to bend a batten around the face of it in profile; mark off the sheer, waterlines, and bottom; lay out these points along a straight line; and, with their half-breadths set out, draw in the back rabbet or half-siding of the face of the main stem.

On the other hand, as mentioned, you would probably skip the pattern bit and apply the half-breadths directly to the face of the stem itself after it has been cut to the profile pattern. You could also take the offsets of the bearding line directly to the stem.

Picking Up

After so many pages and drawings, it is surely long past time to pick up patterns and moulds of this simple little skiff. A writer can't help wondering how many readers of the type bursting with nervous energy may have bolted the patch and gone to put a boat together. But I have tried to consider the reflective types, too, the ones who are curious to know all they can about the subject, for they can get just as impatient with over-simplification as the others can with anything more than enough to get going. After 40 years of lofting, I find that those who barge ahead sometimes wind up running the show, and that other times, so do those who can't start until they understand it. The only sure thing is that each puts on a very different show, while the hardest thing to predict is who *really* will "inherit the earth."

Picking up the lines from the floor and transferring them onto wooden moulds, parts, or templates of parts is no big deal, but some surprisingly elaborate systems have been devised to raise the lines to the upper surface of such wooden pieces. One method uses deeply notched pointers nailed to the floor with their points set over the line. When a board is slid underneath the pointers, marks drawn at the pointers' ends give a series of points, which, when connected by a line, duplicates the original line. Another

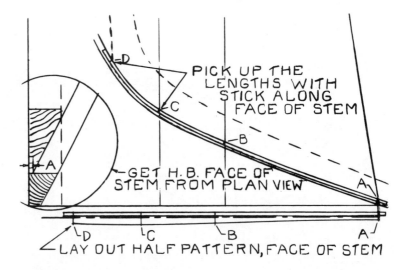

Figure 3-8. *To make a pattern of the stem face, pick up the half-breadths at the points of reference and apply them at their proper lengths along the stem.*

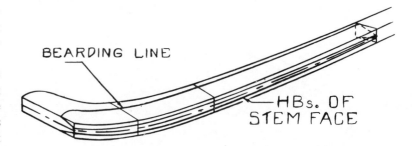

Figure 3-9. *A stem with bearding line and half-breadths marked out.*

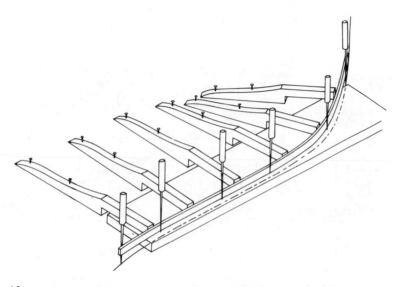

Above: Figure 3-10. *Pickup pointers in use.* **Below: Figure 3-11.** *Other configurations, with battens fixed to the pointers.*

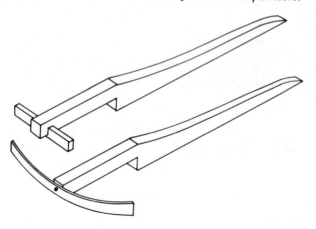

method is to spring a batten and pin it against the pointers' ends so that most of the line can be drawn along it. I have also seen these permanently affixed to a batten.

Another method is to use rocker sticks, which are curved sticks with a hole in each end for picks. To use such sticks, a batten must first be sprung along the line you wish to pick up. When the batten has been set in place with picks, a row of rocker sticks is set up and pinned to it at one end and to the floor at the other end. Then after removing the picks that held the batten while setting it up, the whole thing can be lifted enough so that a board can be slid under it and marked. (*See* Figure 3–12.)

Although I used to prefer the rocker method because it was quick and versatile, I gave it up in favor of the plasterboard nail system. You don't have to use that kind of nail; some types of box nails, or any nail with a thin, sharp-edged head will do. The old blue-steel sheet rock kind was an ideal size and shape, and it was a sorry day for loftsmen when these were replaced by the galvanized nail. To use this system, you simply lay the nail on the floor with its head along the line and tap the head halfway into the floor with a hammer blow. When you have placed them wherever you think they are needed, set a board over the row of them and hammer or stamp it down. When you pick up the board, the line or lines are printed in the board by the other half of the head.

The advantages of the nails are these: you can rapidly set up as many as you think you need (to the point where the print on the board can be almost penciled in or sawn freehand); you can pick up in one impression as many different lines, angles, and curves as you wish; and as you get handy with the nails, you can usually arrange to have most of them stay in the board when you pick it up, so that a batten or straightedge can be laid along them for drawing in the line.

The lines are transferred to the top of the board in the first methods, and to the bottom by the nails, but this shouldn't disturb you, since everything in lofting is symmetrically drawn around a centerline. In building moulds, it is best to pick up a pattern for one side, and then after it is marked out, to nail it to another board and saw out both boards (one for each side) at the same time. The two sides will be identical, provided that the saw blade is normal to its table.

In this skiff, probably the only time you would have use for the above methods of picking up lines would be in picking up patterns of the stem and transom. For such patterns, a single piece of plywood or hardboard is ideal, and with the nails, you can pick up the entire drawing in one move. If the moulds are to be used for building numerous similar boats, it might also be worth making them of a solid sheet of plywood. This is too expensive for building just one boat; for this, all you need is an outline formed by 1″ x 6″ boards. You can simply lay each board against its line on the body plan, mark its ends and cut them, and return it to the loft for assembly. With but a half-section drawn on the floor for each mould, you need to arrange for a couple of points on the opposite side of the centerline in order to position the pieces so that they can be properly assembled. Extend the sheer and bottom lines across the centerline and pop in a pick at the half-breadth of each to complete the section.

When you come to setting up the moulds, you must remember that the skiff's shape is constantly changing along her length. Remember also that the sections represent the hull shape only at the *exact* point of their respective stations. Thus, unless you bevel a mould to fit the planking or stringers, the hull's shape, as depicted by the sections, is represented by the mould *only at one edge of the mould*, not along the mould's entire thickness. In recognition of these facts, you must position the moulds that are forward of the extreme beam on the after side of their station lines, and all after moulds on the forward side of the stations. "Aft forward, and forward aft," the rule says; then the planking

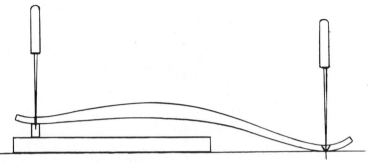

Figure 3-12. *A rocker stick in use.*

Figure 3-13. *Picking up a stem with nails.*

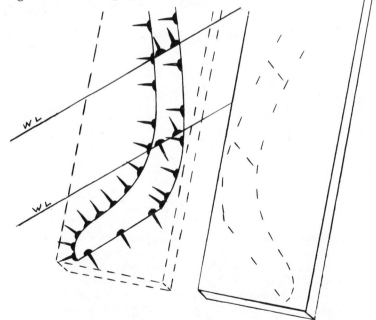

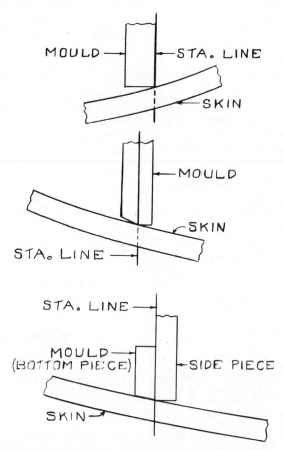

MOULD → ← STA. LINE

← SKIN

←— MOULD

← SKIN

STA. LINE →

STA. LINE →

MOULD (BOTTOM PIECE) → ← SIDE PIECE

SKIN →

Figure 3-14. *The moulds are set up either on or along the station lines. When unbeveled (top), they are set up on the enlarging side of the station. When beveled (middle), they can be set up on the station lines. Moulds built with overlapping pieces (bottom) can straddle the station lines, with the piece toward the end beveled.*

will lie fair on that edge of the mould that is on the station line.

This is not to say that it wouldn't be good to bevel the mould and set it up on the diminishing side of the station. It's sometimes done, but usually only if more than one boat is to be built on the same moulds, for the sharp edges of unbeveled moulds tend to break down after repeated use. As a compromise, you can mark a centerline on the edge of the mould, bevel half of the mould away, and set it up centered on the station line. This method lets you over-bevel the edge, which is easier than trying to get it just right, and it centers the compression of planking, stringers, or ribbands, reducing the tendency of a mould to bow under stress.

Another effect of the angled skin is that cleats or braces used to tie the pieces of a mould together must be kept back from the mould's edges. If this is not possible, they must, at least, be kept on the side facing amidships. In the case of the skiff's station 1 and station 3 moulds, if you fit the side and bottom pieces flush on the floor, cleating them at the bottom corners, and put a cross spall on top of the two side pieces at the sheer, the flush edge next to the floor can be on the station line, with the cleats and cross spall facing away from the ends. This is not as critical with the station 2 mold, as the skiff's sides don't angle in sharply there. If you elect to fasten the bottom piece on top of the side pieces to do away with cleating, you will find that the best station line would be the corner of the side piece that lies next to the bottom piece, or vice-versa, meaning that the station line would be where the boards are face-to-face. With this method, you would have to bevel those parts of the mould that lie on the diminishing side of the station line.

So that's the gist of picking up, except for one more thing. While you have the moulds on the floor, you should not forget to mark them with helpful lines, such as the centerline and sheerline, with any pertinent bevels, and most important, with bold, indelible identification. The mould for station 2 might be labeled like this: *station 2, forward face, top, 5' 11⅜" from stem face*. Nor would it hurt to add *12-foot skiff*, for it is amazing how soon you forget what something is when it has been kicking around for a while, not to mention the fact that only the one who made it knows what it is.

Setting Up

The first test of your lofting comes when you set up the parts you have made. You can head off some frustration and some possible doubts about the parts' accuracy if you make proper preparations before trying to align them. The first consideration is to provide a centerline so that all parts can be kept on the fore-and-aft axis. Another consideration is to lay out the locations of the parts at the exact intervals called for along that centerline, with the station lines normal to it, which will help to keep the moulds squared up. This much you should do whether building your boat upright or upside down, though in many upright setups, the centerline and station lines would be laid out on a prefabricated bottom or keel assembly, which itself would have been set up true relative to a level base. This would not necessarily have to be level fore and aft, though certainly so athwartships, as long as the heights measured the same off a level line as off the baseline.

If, however, you are building the skiff upside down, the centerline and the station lines should be laid out on the floor, or on whatever substitute for a floor you have arranged. If you are building a direct mold for her, the same preparations would still be in order.

There is no way, even with a little skiff like this, that I can cover here all of the possible arrangements for setting up using the wide array of construction methods available to a builder today. However, the principles are the same in all methods, and the following outline of procedures might serve as a reminder.

1. *Identification of and useful markings for the parts*
   a) What part it is
   b) Positioning lines: plumb and level or waterlines, stations, sheerline, and centerlines—vertical, horizontal, and up and down stem and transom
   c) Heights, distances from . . .
   d) Which side is forward, which side is aft
   e) Which side is on the station line
2. *Provide a base for the parts*
   According to the setup, this might include the following: blocking, a strongback, horses, a spider of boards to nail to (on a cement floor), legs, and braces (possibly from the walls or overhead).
3. *Lay out a locating plan on the floor or supporting structure*
   a) A centerline
   b) Station lines
   c) Bow and stern perpendiculars, and/or locating marks for the feet of stem and transom
4. *Set up parts*
   a) Start in the middle and thoroughly brace the widest mould after plumbing it carefully both ways and "horning" it. (Horning means to check that a part is normal to the centerline by getting long, equal measurements to similar points on each half of the part from a point on the centerline well forward or aft.)
   b) Set up adjacent parts, working toward the ends; tie each mould to the last with sticks nailed to each, plumbing and bracing as needed; check the spacing as you go.
   c) Carefully horn the transom and plumb the stem.
   d) Replace the spacing sticks with one continuous ribband or stringer, or more if called for by the setup.

Now, step back, take a good look, try a batten here and there for fairness, congratulate yourself, turn her over to the boatbuilders, or put on a boatbuilding hat. She's lofted, picked up, and set up.

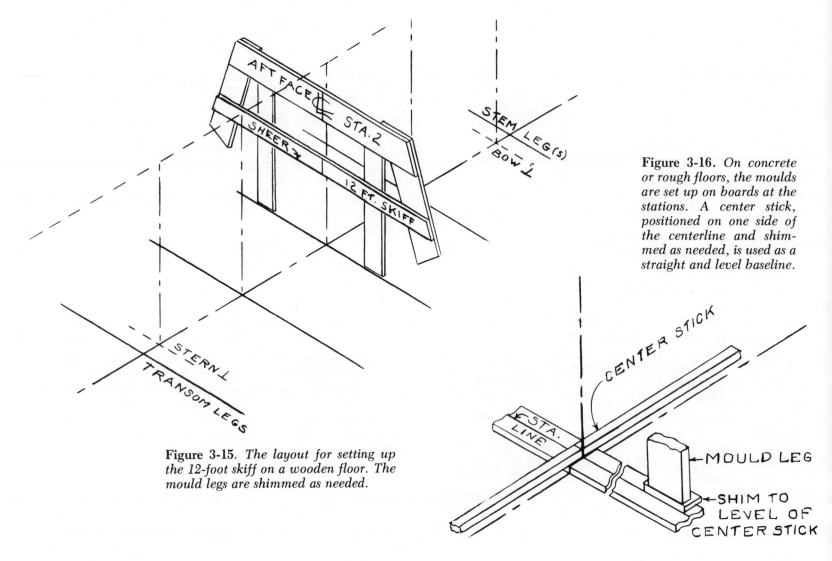

Figure 3-16. *On concrete or rough floors, the moulds are set up on boards at the stations. A center stick, positioned on one side of the centerline and shimmed as needed, is used as a straight and level baseline.*

Figure 3-15. *The layout for setting up the 12-foot skiff on a wooden floor. The mould legs are shimmed as needed.*

4 / Minimum Lofting a Skiff

For a number of reasons, including just not caring to be as technical about it, you might want to build the 12-foot skiff with the least possible lofting. If so, you can do without a large part of what was put forth in the last two chapters. Ironically, the more versed you are in lofting, the more shortcuts you can devise without making a lot of extra work for yourself whittling on parts you could have cut right the first time if you had spent a little time drawing them. That is to say that shortcuts work best for the loftsmen with the most know-how—just like borrowing is easiest for those with the most money. Anyway, when you know your way around the loft, you should be able to build a good skiff with much less drawing.

For what you will be doing, you need no bigger loft than a "scrive board," the traditional name for a body plan-size board on which a vessel's moulds or frames can be drawn out and assembled. Sometimes the scrive board is set up at the building site after a full lofting job has been done, but other times drawing the body plan on it is just about all the lofting a vessel gets. Our skiff's minimum lofting starts with drawing her half-sections on the scrive board, and the only items you must draw are the baseline, centerline, and the sides and bottom at stations 1, 2, and 3—just enough to make the three moulds.

You should skip drawing the transoms and stem here because the body plan views of these do not indicate their true lengths. Minimum lofting, by definition, uses only views from which you can *directly* pick up essential parts or information. You also should not bother to put in the sheer and chine lines or keel and skeg, since the first two add nothing buildable to the stations they connect, and the keel and skeg can be more quickly laid out right on the boards from which they will be cut.

To get patterns of the stem and transom, you will have to draw the ends of the profile, which contain the only "true" views of these parts. You will have to set up bow and stern perpendiculars near the right and left edges of the scrive board and draw the profiles of stem and transom in their proper relation, heightwise, to the body plan and base. This will automatically provide you with heights for setting her up and will put the two profiles in position for some projections or partial views that you might choose to draw to get shape or beveling information.

All of the above is done directly from the table of offsets and the lines plan. Without the long lines, you cannot fair anything except the stem's curves as you draw them. However, you can compare what you draw with the lines plan for the similarity of curves and angles and spaces between section lines in the body plan. A critical eye will often catch some errors this way. Such study is worthwhile, for it may save you from having to work the parts later, should you set them up and find them disagreeing with one another.

To loft the transom, you must draw a half-pattern just as was done in Chapter 2. Mark off the bottom and sheer heights on the

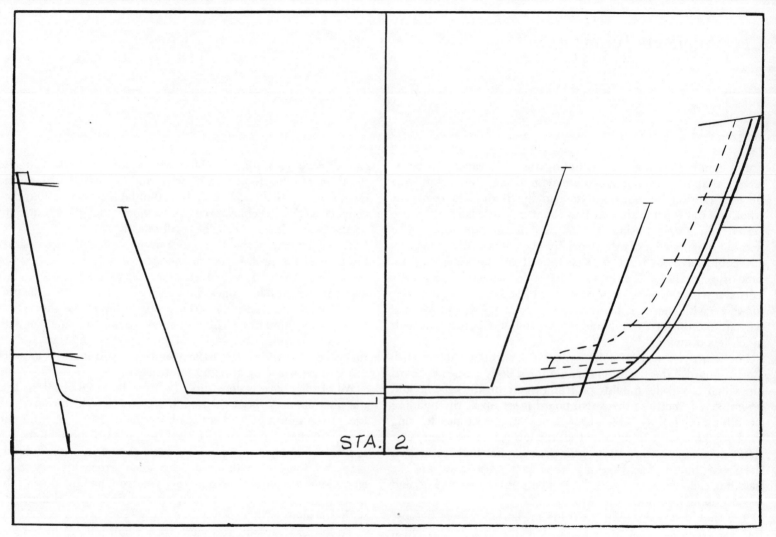

STA. 2

Figure 4-1. *A scrive board for the 12-foot skiff, with three stations and stem and profile.*

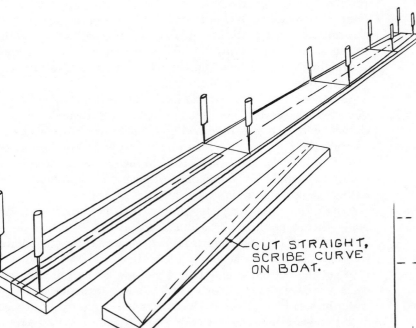

CUT STRAIGHT,
SCRIBE CURVE
ON BOAT.

Figure 4-2. *Laying out the keel and skeg directly on the stock. The keel should be laid out around a centerline and should be cut extra long to allow for the curve of the bottom.*

Figure 4-3. *In comparing the lofting to the plan, note that the section at station 2 has less height than the same section has in the plans (see* arrow*). In this case, the offset for the station 2 sheer half-breadth was mis-read as 2-2-1 instead of 2-1-2 as given.*

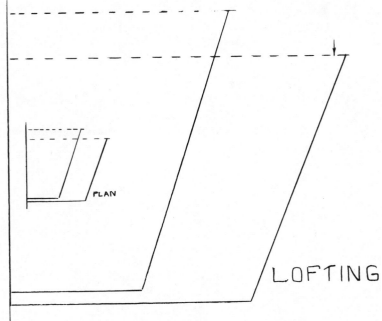

PLAN

LOFTING

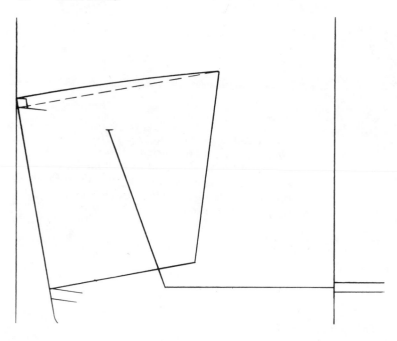

Figure 4-4. *The half-face of the transom is drawn against the transom in profile.*

profile; then project them normal to the transom line and set off their half-breadths. When it comes to drawing the curved top, skip any reference to the body plan and half-breadth views of the transom, and simply draw the curve you want full length against a straight line, and then transfer half of it directly to the half-pattern drawing.

You obviously have drawn nothing thus far from which to take the transom's bevels, but you are lucky in that angles do not change with the size of drawings. This means that you can measure them right on the lines plan if you wish. You have to be careful to take the lines' angles close to the transom, and it helps to draw a straight line on the nearest part of the bottom or side, letting the curve go as it sweeps away.

If you are too fussy to simply lift the angles off the plan—there's nothing like a full-size drawing—you can fairly quickly lay off two station lines properly spaced to the right of the transom, mark off the heights of the bottom, and draw enough of it to get the bottom angle. To get the side angles full-size, you need to draw some half-breadth lines. Remembering that waterlines give you truer angles in this boat, you might as well drop two waterlines into the body plan, extend them to the transom profile, and set off their half-breadths on the same stations used for the bottom line. You should remember to locate the half-breadth line that crosses the transom at the point where the waterline intersects the transom in profile. You must get the length of this line from the transom half-pattern after projecting the waterline across the half-pattern from the same intersection. When drawn in, this line will form an angle with the side from which you can determine the proper bevel for the transom sides.

Now, if the size of your scrive board doesn't allow enough space for two stations, you can leave out station 2 and put in station 3½ (as shown in Figure 4–5) to get the third point needed to generate the line's proper curve. Should you find it necessary to do this, you need only take your scale rule and triangle, draw the half station in the lines plan, scale the offsets that relate to it, and set the points out on the scrive board.

Draw the stem in profile much as it was drawn in the full lofting. You should include the sheer and a bit of the bottom and bottom planking, which you can get with heights and angles from the table and the plan.

To get the sections of the false stem and main stem, you can project the sheer and bottom from the profile down to half-breadth drawings and then lift the angles that sheer and bottom half-breadths form with the centerline from the plan. But what about the stem's sections between top and bottom? It might be a good idea to have at least one intermediate section, say at about a third of the way up the stem. If you're so inclined, a waterline run through this area, then drawn in its half-breadth view, will do very nicely—much as it was done in Chapter 2, but with dropped-in stations or half stations this time.

However, the quickest way with this boat is to go with sheer and bottom sections only. To do this, first pick up a pattern of the main stem from the profile and cut out the stem. Then draw a bearding line having roughly the same curve as the stem face from the bearding line point at the sheer (which you have found in the sheer cross-section) down to the bottom bearding line point. You must also take the back rabbet half-breadth from the sheer in plan view to the face of the main stem and draw parallel lines with a straightedge batten (thin but wide enough not to bend edgewise) bent around the face. Finally, you can create a false stem piece the same way, laying it out on the lumber.

A fair question would be how you know that the curve of the face will work for the bearding line. Well, logic says that if the stem were straight on this straight-sectioned boat, the bearding line would be a straight line between the point at the sheer and one at the bottom. All we have done, in effect, is to bow a straight stem and bearding line outward a little, maintaining their relationship with like curves. In truth, the skiff's lines are drawn out

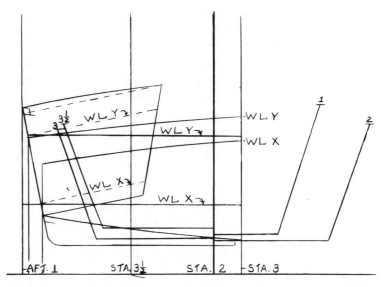

Above: Figure 4-5. *Scrive board with stations 3 and 3½ drawn in. These additions enable waterlines X and Y to be drawn, from which bevels can be taken for the transom side.* **Below: Figure 4-6.** *When the stem is shaped using a faked bearding line, a sliver of excess wood will have to be trimmed off during fitting on the boat.*

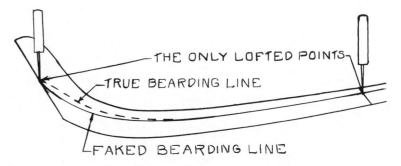

longer by the outward curve to a slightly flatter angle than the straight stem would have had. A few swipes of the plane will quickly make the stem section right, for in such a case, the difference between the faked bearding line and the true one will always be one involving excess wood that can be planed down.

At this point, you have ample information to pick up and set up the boat, as described in the last chapter. The resulting boat will not be inferior in any way as long as you use your good eye to check fairness as you go and have the patience to stop and sort out any details that don't seem to go together just right. The key to success in this time-saving method is to spend a few moments now and then to study and fair the building job as you go along.

The lofting of a round-bottomed design differs from the skiff in that, no matter how you slice it, the boat's surface appears as a curved line. Curves and more curves are what you'll be drawing and they certainly make for the most beautiful boats.

The example I chose to illustrate this chapter is the ketch *Araminta*, the smallest in the famous line of L. Francis Herreshoff-designed clipper-bowed ketches, which he sometimes referred to as developments of the schooner *America* hull type. From the 72-foot *Ticonderoga* on down, they are all beauties and wonderful performers, but as a masterpiece in the art of refined sailboat design, the 33-foot *Araminta*, with her breathtaking low sheer, graceful ends, and fine lines, has no peer. Those of us who have had the joy of sailing her can testify that she is truly, as her designer once remarked, "a boat to show off with." When a boat sails beautifully, she is a pleasure; when you are also entranced, just watching her ride at her mooring any time of day in any weather, as I am by *Araminta*, she's pure joy! There's nothing like having a beautiful set of lines to keep your batteries charged during the lofting process.

You can't draw curves without laying down at least three points—often you will need considerably more—so you should have 20 to 35 picks on hand. Also, you will need nice, long board of clear stock for making battens of different shapes and sizes.

After preparing a floor longer than the boat and a couple of feet wider than her height in profile, you should set up the grid, which consists of a straight line view of all the waterlines, stations, buttock lines, and diagonals. This is a design where the LWL (load waterline, also often known as the DWL or designed waterline) serves as the baseline. As Herreshoff notes under the table of offsets, "Heights [are] above and below L.W.L." So you should start by putting the LWL on the floor, making sure that you have planned its location so that there will be enough space for what will be drawn above and below it. Since the height of the profile includes 5 feet of draft below the LWL and 3' ⅞" to the highest point of the sheer above it, the profile needs just over 8 feet of floor width.

All this is fine, but where are you going to draw the plan view, which will be one half of the 8' 6" beam, or 4' 3" wide? You would need a floor 13 to 14 feet wide to draw it clear of the profile as the designer did. Yet, even if you have plenty of room for this, you'd save a lot of time by drawing this view superimposed on the profile to some extent, keeping all three views within easy reach. And that goes for the half-breadths of the diagonals, too, which are usually laid down under the centerline used for the plan view. Perhaps the handiest location for the plan view and diagonals of this boat would be off a centerline that is an even 6 feet below the LWL. This would keep the half-breadths of the keel clear of the keel's profile and thus eliminate confusion; yet it would allow you to use some waterlines of the profile for buttock lines of the plan view, since both are spaced one foot apart. You

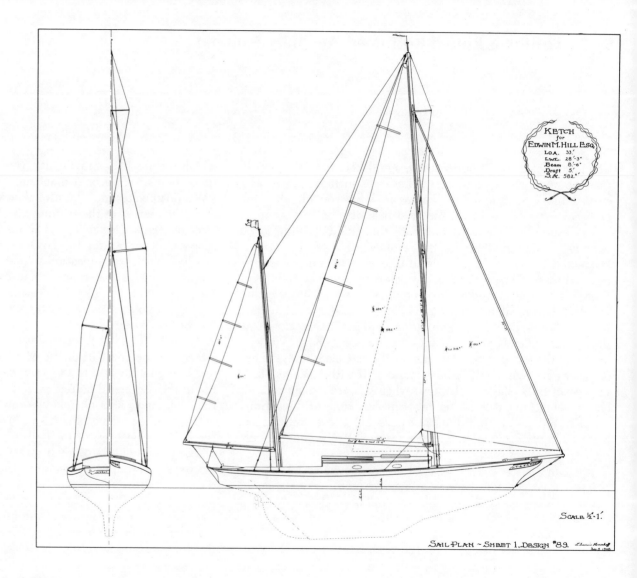

Right: Figure 5-1. Araminta's *sail plan*.

Opposite: Figure 5-2. Araminta's *lines plan*.

KETCH
for
Edwin M. Hill Esq.
L.O.A. 33'
L.W.L. 28'-3"
Beam 8'-6"
Draft 5'
S.A. 582'

Scale ½=1'

Sail Plan ~ Sheet 1, Design #89.

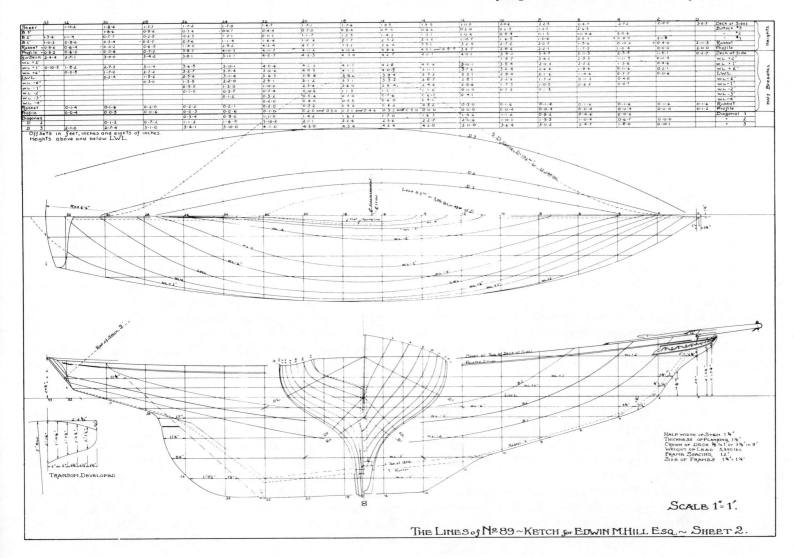

The Lines of Nº 89 ~ Ketch for Edwin M. Hill Esq. ~ Sheet 2.

Scale 1" = 1'.

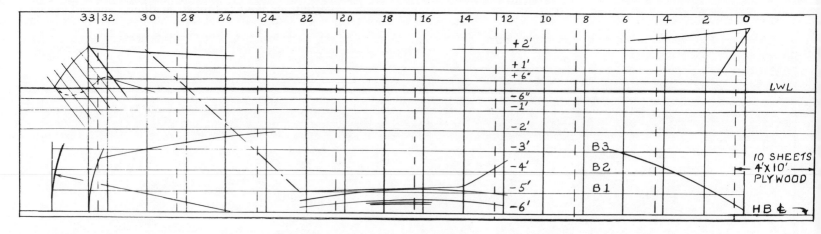

Figure 5-3. *The grid layout for lofting* Araminta.

could also use the same set of station lines extended downward to this –6′ WL (minus six foot waterline). The grid for such a layout would look like that shown in Figure 5–3.

Note from the drawing that I have kept the station lines clear of the plywood sheet joints, using an uneven measurement that also clears any half stations you might draw. There is nothing more annoying than trying to establish points along cracks, for they refract lines, won't hold picks, and split out along the edges.

Other possible locations for basing the plan view include almost any waterline. The LWL is often used as the centerline, with the half-breadth waterlines and diagonals set off either above it or below it. Drawing the plan view in this manner concentrates the lines, putting the many endings of the long lines right in the midst of their companion points in the profile and body plans. Should you go this route, it is obvious that there will be plenty of confusion, whether the plan view is above or below the LWL, so a different color pencil will be invaluable.

The body plan of this boat is drawn around station 17, this being one of those designs whose stations are designated as a distance from the foremost point of the hull. You should draw in the buttock lines and diagonals that flank the body plan centerline as part of the grid. Buttocks and diagonals are lengthwise slices of the hull whose locations are chosen by the designer as best serving his need to fair certain features of the lines. But for convenience, he will often use spacings for buttocks that fall on, or are even divisions of, station and waterline spacings. The resulting plan is handy, neat, and simple.

Diagonals usually are drawn as normal to the skin of the boat as possible. These lines are the most useful of the long lines (buttocks, waterlines, and diagonals) for determining the fairness of a set of lines: due to their squareness to the skin, they give a much more precise "fix" than lines that intersect the skin at more oblique angles, as waterlines and buttocks often do. A favorite location for one of these diagonals is at a 45-degree angle downward from the LWL, which is certainly normal to the deadrise of most boats somewhere along the bottom—sure enough, there is one of these in *Araminta*. For convenience, designers often choose crossings of the grid lines for the terminations of diagonals. If not, they will give heights up the centerline and distances out on a waterline or on the baseline. *Araminta*'s diagonals all end at crossings, and although her lines are erased in a margin around the body plan for clarity, the designer has left segments of the lower endings on the crossings of waterlines and station lines.

The sequence for lofting most round-bottomed boats should be the following:

1. Grid
2. Profile
3. Half-breadth outline (sheerline, stem, keel, deadwood, horn timber)
4. Body plan
5. Long lines
6. Transom
7. Details of parts to be picked up—stem, keel, sternpost, horn timber, floors, rudder, aperture, shaft line (and related details), stringers and beds, mast steps, etc.
8. Deductions (or add-ons) for planking
9. Floor line, if building upside down
10. Moulds and patterns

Some boats have critical features that should be drawn as soon as possible, with the rest of the boat drawn around them. *Araminta*, as you shall see later, is such a boat.

Start *Araminta*'s profile with the "sheer," as it says at one end of the table of offsets, or "top of deck at side," as it says at the other. Right away, as you put a pick in station 0 at 3-0-7 above the LWL, you might get an uneasy feeling. Isn't there a bowsprit projecting out partly below the point where 0 intersects the sheer, and doesn't the stem appear to terminate at some point forward

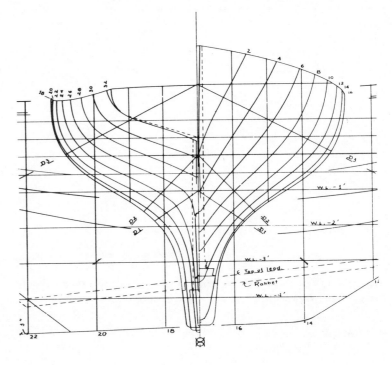

Figure 5-4. *Araminta's* *diagonals end at grid line intersections.*

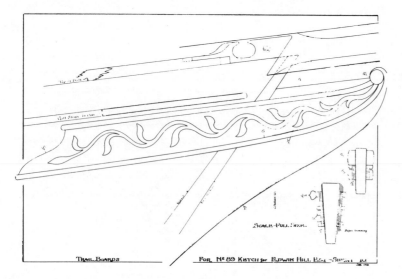

Figure 5-5. *This detailed drawing of* Araminta's *stemhead shows the forward termination of the deck at side line.*

of 0? Just where *is* the forward end of "top of deck at side"? There are some dotted lines in the middle of the bowsprit in the profile, and some dimensions forward of 0 in the plan view that might give you a pretty good idea, but rather than start off on the wrong foot, you should get out the construction plan, then Sheet 10, which is a full-size drawing of the trailboards and the stemhead details.

Now it should be clear: the bowsprit is notched over the deck and stemhead, and some of the latter does project forward of 0, so the sheerline hangs out forward from there the 2¼" indicated on the plan view. Also, make a mental note that you should scratch this station line deeply into the side and top of the stem, and point out to the builders that in this boat the bow perpendicular (station 0) is there and not at the stem face, as in most boats whose stations are designated by their distance aft of it. Later, when the bowsprit covers the top of the stem, the foremost point of the top of deck at side from which you can measure will be just about where station 0 is; that is probably why the designer used this unusual arrangement. At least it's logical.

When you get to the stern, you find that the last height given is at station 32. Apparently Herreshoff didn't feel it necessary to give a height for station 33, so you'll just have to draw the sheerline 6" or more past 32, where the top of the transom will intersect it. Any sign of droop should be eliminated by pushing up the tail of the batten slightly, for there is nothing worse than a flattened curve at either end of a springy sheerline. It will bother the eye as soon as it comes into view.

When you are satisfied with the sheer, you might be wise to move the batten down and draw the painted stripe shown on the profile. With everything at hand, it will never be easier to do than now, nor will you get a better chance to study its fairness and relationship to the sheer without the interference of a host of other lines. You will have to scale it, as no offsets are given, but you can get the forward end from Sheet 10 of the construction plans and an overall impression of how the designer wanted it to look from the sail plan. Then when it finally comes time to put the batten on the planked-up hull, you'll have some good offsets to work with—and you may be glad of that if the boat is in a crowded place where you can't get away to look at it. Note that the designer has accentuated the boat's sheer by giving the cove stripe a little more curve than the sheer and a quicker curve at the after end. As naval architect Walter McInnis once said to me, "Everything on a hull should have an upward sweep toward the ends if you want a good looking boat." You only have to look at his designs to believe it.

As you turn to the "½ w Deck," or "Deck at side," in the half-breadth part of the table, you will see that there are offsets for every station, including 33, which is past the transom intersection. From this you know you can get the half-breadth curve of the sheer without too much trouble. However, in the short space from station 0 to the tip of the stem, the line must pass through a cluster of three points: station 0, given in the offsets as 0-2-7; the half-breadth of the stem face, given in the plan view as 1⁵⁄₁₆"; and the rabbet, given as 0-1-6 (the half-width of the stem) in the table, and dimensioned as 1" forward of 0 in the plan view.

Now before you have lofted many boats, a situation like this might be cause for alarm. Unless the lines have already been corrected, the chances of a batten negotiating all three of these closely spaced points, or even two of them, are pretty slim. When the picks are in, you may well find that the batten fairs through 0 and the face of the stem within reason, but that the point for the rabbet is too far inboard to make sense. Since you wouldn't want to make either the face of the stem or the half-breadth at 0 narrower than specified in order to connect with the rabbet at 1" forward of 0, you will just have to move the rabbet line forward about ½" until its fixed half-breadth intersects with the sheerline. This

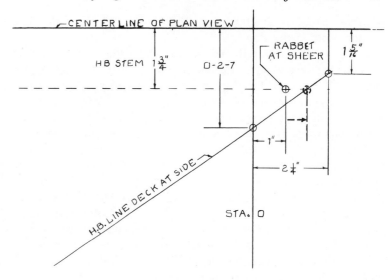

Figure 5-6. *The rabbet, as given in the plans, does not fall on the deck at side line. To bring it into line, its position must be shifted forward.*

shouldn't cause trouble later since there seems to be enough room to play with on the stem.

With that detail sorted out, you can draw the half-breadth of the deck at side and go on to complete the profile. Taking heights from the table and the supplementary dimensions given on the plan, draw the profile of stem, keel, rudder, "nightcap" (the almost triangular piece over the rudder, so named by old builders because its shape is reminiscent of a nightcap), counter, and transom. At the bow you will want to draw the profile of the "false piece" carefully. This is crucial to the looks of the boat, and was obviously important to Herreshoff, who gave it several extra offsets and provided a full-size drawing of it on Sheet 10 as well. Note that the face of the stem has a half-inch notch starting at WL +1′ into which the false piece fits, which is to say that the face of the stem follows the profile up to WL +1′, jogs in ½″, then continues in a straight line to the top. You should hold this part straight to ease the fitting of the false piece to it.

You will then want to draw in the centerline of the rudder stock as well as the profile of the rudder and nightcap. The position of the rudder stock will be needed later on, for the waterlines from –2′ down change direction at that point (which is the after end of the deadwood and rudderpost, combined here in a single piece of timber). Horizontal offsets are given for the rudder stock centerline along WL +1′ and the bottom of the keel. As you continue up the counter or horn timber, you find that the designer has faired the profile, the rabbet, and the buttock lines right out to station 33. He hasn't taken any chances of your getting any unwanted bumps or hollows in her run.

As meticulous as he has been so far, however, Herreshoff has made some omissions, which you should now discover. He hasn't given you the distance that the bottom of the rudder is above the bottom of the keel (which scales 1″). And even the most sanguine loftsman will have a distracted moment when he goes to draw the transom profile, for there is a height given at station 33 for the top, but there is no dimension for the intersection of a hypothetical transom extension with the LWL. Shucks!

Search as you may, there is no clue, and as soon as you are satisfied that it was an oversight, scale the plan to find the missing dimension. This comes out to 16″ abaft station 30 and about 8¼″ forward of station 32, indicating that the paper is distorted, since the two measurements should total 24″. If you check a couple of other station spacings, you will see that some of them are a bit off, some ¼″ bigger, some ¼″ smaller. Even though that's no big deal, you may find this to be disturbing if you have an orderly mind. You might want to measure the actual angle the transom makes with the LWL. This comes out to 51 degrees on the nose. Now that's something you can live with, and what's more, when you draw the situation out on the floor full-size you will find that a 51-degree line off the LWL up to the 24½″ height on station 33 will be just about 16″ abaft station 30.

Your next job is to draw the backbone's half-breadths in the plan view from the stemhead to the bottom of the transom. The face of the stem is well dimensioned and should be no problem, but as it turns down to the keel, you see that the half-breadth is 0-0-0 for two stations, which can only mean that the leading edge comes to a point there, albeit a blunt or rounded one. Then, along the bottom of the keel, two half-breadths are given on each station, one for that part of the bottom of the keel that is to remain flat and one for the edge or corner of the keel if it were not rounded off. This second set of dimensions is represented by a dotted line called a "fairing line" by Herreshoff and a "ghost line" by some others. It is needed to tie the lower ends of the station sections into a fair keel; so you should draw and fair both lines.

There will be no trouble following the half-breadths from here to the stern once you realize that they apply to the bottom and after edges of keel, rudder, and horn timber. The line they form is

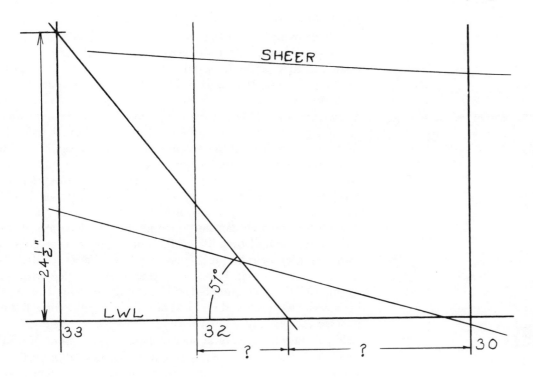

SHEER

LWL

24½"

51°

33

32

?   ?

30

Left: Figure 5-7. *The missing transom offset can be found either by measuring the transom angle or by scaling the plans. The former is a better method, since any distortion in the plans can throw off scaled measurements.*

Below: Figure 5-8. *The bottom of the station sections are tied together by a fairing line.*

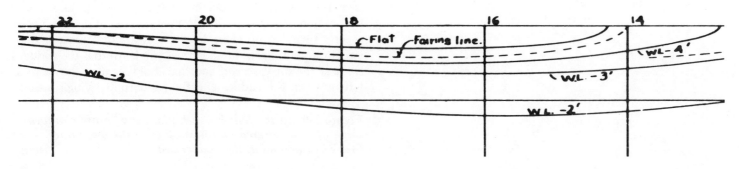

22   20   18   16   14

Flat   Fairing line.

WL -4'

WL -3'

WL -2

WL. -2'

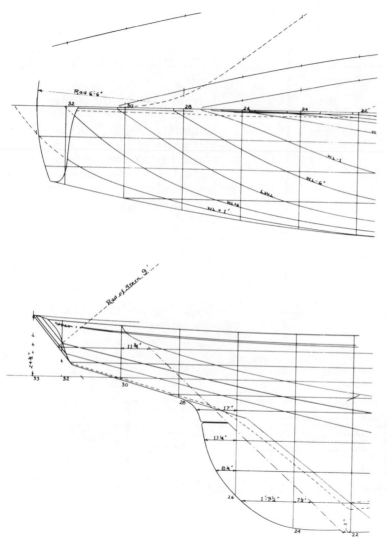

the "profile" referred to in the table (not to be confused with the profile drawing). You can carry this right along as a continuation of the keel's fairing line that narrows from 1″ off the centerline at station 22 to ⅜″ at 26, back out to ¾″ at 28, and down to ½″ again by the time you get to station 32. But you are not quite through with drawing the half-breadth "profile," because as mentioned earlier, the waterlines in way of the rudderpost and rudder do not fair out to the end of the rudder in this boat; there is a break or slight angle in them at the aft edge of the rudderpost. Therefore, you should draw in the half-breadth of that after edge so that waterlines –2′ to –4′ can fair to it. Projected to the plan view, this line will extend from 3″ aft of station 22 to just over 3″ aft of station 26, depending on precisely where the top of the rudder and bottom of nightcap lie. Since neither the location of these parts nor the half-breadth of the rudderpost's after edge are shown in plan or table, it is time to get out the rest of the plans and do some research. When a designer omits so much critical information from the lines plan, it is certainly to be hoped that it is because he has provided it elsewhere. (If he hasn't, you will have to scale the plans as a last resort.)

If you unroll the several sheets of plans, you should find the following: a section drawing of station 26 tucked under the aft end of the construction profile on the construction plan, a full-size drawing of this area in profile (Sheet 9), and a written description or set of specifications composed of seven typewritten sheets, keyed to numbers in circles scattered through the construction plan. From these sources you learn that the rudder is 2″ thick at the forward end and that the designer wants a ¼″ space left between the rudder and the rudderpost, which means that

Figure 5-9. *In the half-breadth plan, the "profile" appears as a series of steps formed by the endings of the waterlines. Note the break in the lines at the rudderpost.*

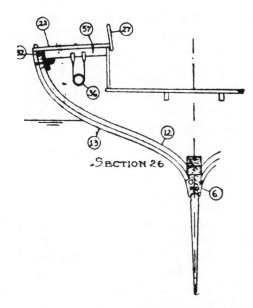

. SECTION 26

Above: Figure 5-10. *Section drawing of station 26 from the construction drawing. The numbers refer to construction specifications outlined by Herreshoff on a separate specifications list.*

Below: Figure 5-11. *Sheet 9, details of the nightcap and the top of the rudder.*

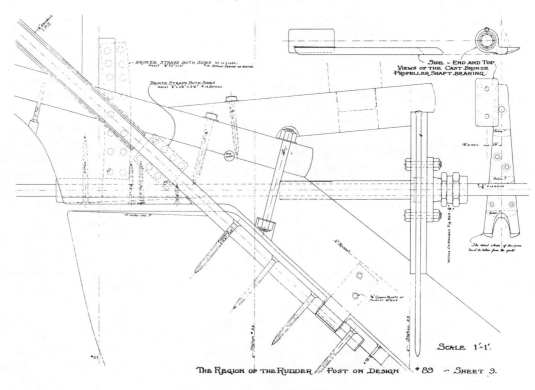

THE REGION OF THE RUDDER POST ON DESIGN #89 ~ SHEET 9.

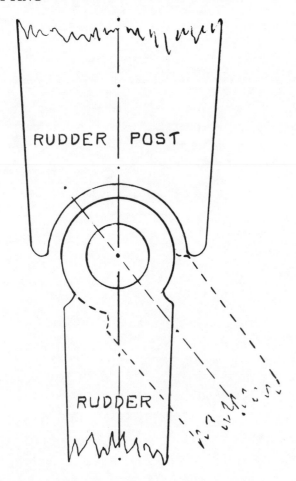

RUDDER | POST

RUDDER

Figure 5-12. *A full-sized sectional drawing of the rudderpost will determine the amount of clearance necessary to achieve the maximum desired rudder angle.*

the after edge of the rudderpost will contain an approximately semicircular hollow 2½″ wide to receive the rudder. Therefore, you might decide to establish 3″ as the overall width of the after edge. As close as I can tell, that's what it scales in the detail section of station 26, and I think that ¼″ is thin enough for the edges of the hollowed after face. If the joiners dare plane it thinner, let 'em. You can also figure out from Sheet 9 just where the designer wants the top of the rudder and the bottom of the "wood fairing piece" that I have been calling the nightcap.

It is a good idea to draw yourself a full section of the post and rudder, normal to the stock's centerline, so that you can determine whether a given arrangement will work best to allow the rudder enough swing, while giving you the fairest transition across the joint. *Araminta*'s arrangement shows the need with wood to have good clearance (for painting if nothing else) and to avoid fragility.

In all cases, you need to be sure that the rudder can turn enough to either side for good steering without jamming. How much is enough depends on the type of boat. A heavy boat with a long keel can't turn a very tight circle, and turning the rudder too far will only cause it to stall at some angle in the 35-to-45–degree range. On the other hand, a light, shallow hull with a daggerboard or a fin keel might be able to react favorably to 50 or 60 degrees of rudder angle. You may find that the steerer specified has stops at a certain angle, so that your only concern as a loftsman is to draw an arrangement that can turn that far. The designer might have a maximum angle in mind, but he will rarely indicate this on the plans. If approached on the subject he might be one of those who says, "I'll look into it." This is one of the hazards of the business, and a conscientious loftsman can waste a lot of time waiting for answers, at least until he gets enough experience to take the bull by the horns when he can't get anything but bull on the horn.

Before you go on to draw the body plan, look over the lines to see whether you will need the rabbet line for the lower endings of

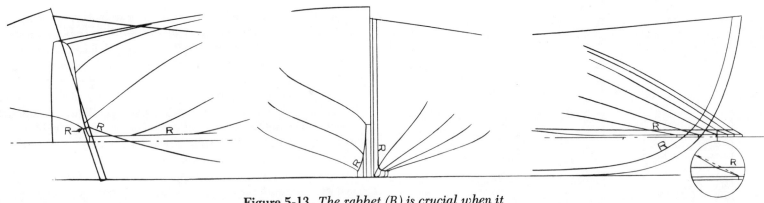

Figure 5-13. *The rabbet (R) is crucial when it is a shape-determining line, as it is in these plans.*

the station sections. In a boat whose stem, keel, and horn timber are slab sided, you certainly would have to draw the rabbet line: as the point where the shape of the hull terminates, it is all important in that kind of construction. In fact, in the past when the intention was to use the same sided dimension for all of the backbone members, many builder's half models were rabbet line models.

In more refined designs drawn with wooden construction in mind, and in almost all current plastic and metal boats, the lines are faired to the face of the stem, to a ghost line, and/or to various radii along the centerline. In such wooden boats, the rabbet line is glossed over, while in the metal or plastic boats it is nonexistent. In all such cases, points other than the rabbet along the profile are the termination of the lines.

Now in *Araminta* there are some lines faired to the face of the backbone members, as at the top of the stem, rudderpost, and

horn timber (labeled the "after keel" by the designer). But the leading edge of the lower stem and "fore keel" are rounded off, so it looks as though you will need the rabbet line as a controlling point at least on stations 4 to 12. What the heck, it won't take too long to run around the profile and the length of the plan view with the rabbet's heights and half-breadths, and if you want, you can skip the half-breadths of any parts where the lines are faired to the face of the member, since the profile half-breadths take precedence there and the rabbet may have to move a little, just as you discovered when you did the half-breadth of the sheer. Not that you can be blamed for being in a hurry to get to the drawing of the body plan. To anyone with an eye for a nice shape this next move is going to be a real pleasure!

In laying down the sections, start with station 2 and go right through the lot of them, one by one, to the stern. The offsets for the sheer and the half-breadth "profile," or the rabbet (whichever

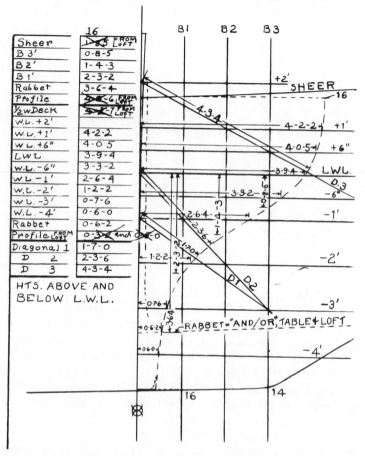

Figure 5-14. *The body plan sections are laid down from measurements in the table of offsets, using waterlines, buttocks, and diagonals as references. Following the rule that "a fair line supersedes any given measurement," those offsets that have already been laid down in other views are picked up from the lofting rather than from the table.*

controls the lower end of the section) should be picked up from your lofting with pickup sticks; all of the offsets in between should come from the table of offsets. Buttock lines, diagonals, and every other point in the column under the station you're doing should be "plugged in."

With picks set at the appropriate points, take a nice long, limber batten and pin it against your picks. When possible, this should be a full-length batten, because then you can study the whole section at once. Should you be lofting a boat with a very hard bilge or an acute reverse turn down to the keel, this may not be practicable, even with an hourglassed or tapered batten. Where overlaps are necessary, they should take place in the straightest parts of the section. Anyway, for a curvaceous body plan where a thin batten is needed, hard wood is better than soft wood; some of the plastics work very well; and for really tight bends, tempered steel, such as a piece of bandsaw blade, is a lifesaver.

What do you do if a point or two seem quite out of place so that the line won't fair through all the points? For now, don't get too upset. A little tinkering will usually show which point is causing the trouble, and if several seem to be in slight disagreement, you might average them as best you can. Here are some general rules for sorting out points in disaccord: the offsets of lines crossing the section most squarely are more to be believed than oblique crossings; similarity to the plan is an important gauge of which curve is the right one, as is similarity of the spaces between sections; and even the shape of the triangle cut off at the corner of a grid rectangle is a clue. If you have trouble with the same long line or set of long lines as you come to each section, it may be that the designer took its offsets at a different time than the others and the plan changed in size in the meantime. In such cases, the error will be progressively larger as the offsets get longer.

With all this in mind, get all of the sections drawn as best you can, knowing that they may be subject to adjustment as you draw the long lines. When you get to the long lines, it will help if you have circled any points in the body plan that you decided to bypass as being "out" when drawing the fairest section line as you see it. It often happens that the long lines will show that an adjacent point or two are the ones at fault, and it will save a lot of checking back and forth to the table if you know which were the "given" points as you adjust the curve. Before leaving the body plan, cap the sections with the sheer, since it has been faired. It probably isn't worthwhile to fuss with the rounding of the sections' lower ends at keel and stem until you have faired everything down to this area.

Using the information that you have drawn in thus far, you can now develop the curved versions of the waterlines and the buttocks in the half-breadth and the profile views respectively. The ball is in your court from now on, and you should only refer to the table of offsets if it appears that you may have made a mistake in reading it the first time or to correct the table when you have proven it wrong. The heights or half-breadths of these long lines should be transferred from the sections in the body plan to the profile and plan views via pickup sticks.

The endings of the buttocks and waterlines can be gotten by projecting their grid-line points of intersection with the vessel's outline to the view in which these lines are missing. In this case, the endings of the waterlines in the plan view—where they meet the face of the stem or stern—are directly below their intersections with the profile in the profile view. Conversely, the endings of the buttocks in the profile view are directly above their straight-line intersections with the "profile" of the plan view (and at the same height as their intersections with the sheer in the body plan).

The endings of the diagonals are quite different, and I must confess to having drawn them wrong for years before designer Carl Alberg said very diplomatically, "That's a nice job of lofting, but let me show you how to draw the diagonal endings." The thing that throws you off about diagonals is that their half-breadths are not measured horizontally or vertically, but at an angle (down the angled line in the body plan to the intersection in question), and the curved long line you develop is what you would see looking down *normal* to the plane of the diagonal, rather than down on it *vertically*. Therefore, the line you develop should always be wider than the part of the boat it intersects. Looking at it this way, you should be able to see why a diagonal ending at the stem face is wider than the half-breadth of the stem face viewed horizontally or vertically. (*See* Figure 5–16.)

Now that you have seen how to draw the diagonal endings, I should point out that it is not necessary to draw them to achieve a fair hull. In fact, most designers and loftsmen don't project the diagonals to the centerline at all, being interested only in the diagonals' fairness *along* the hull. I have merely used the endings as a vehicle to further your understanding: to understand what the endings look like is to better understand what you are looking at in a diagonal.

You can see from the above that diagonals are of little use in the construction because they do not relate easily to the plumb and level offsets generally used to set up and build a boat. However, they are often used to establish a nice planking or plating line. *Araminta* might plank up very neatly if you took D1 as a dividing line and then divided up the areas above and below it into plank widths. In terms of lofting, diagonals—when drawn as normal to the skin as possible— are the best of all lines for fairing the hull. If you think that an area of the body plan could use additional fairing, you might want to drop in an extra diagonal or two as a check. Herreshoff has *Araminta* pretty well covered with one or another of the three kinds of long lines, so about the only places the most meticulous loftsman might care to add diagonals would be perhaps from waterline –2′ on the centerline to the junctures

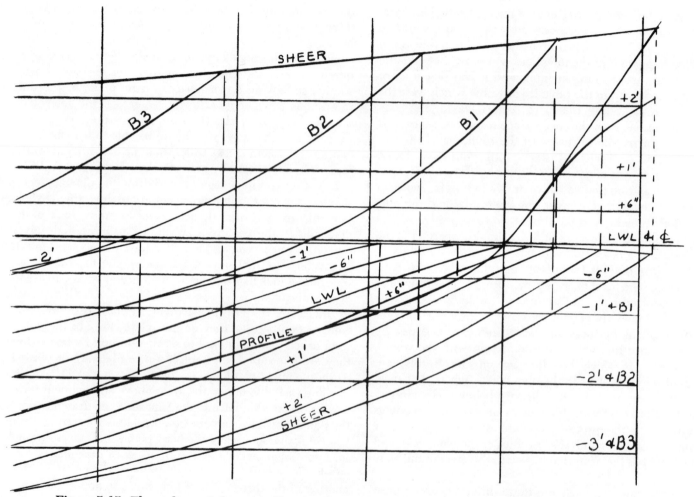

Figure 5-15. *The endings of the curved long lines must be transferred from one view to another: buttock endings in profile come from the plan view; waterline endings are projected down from profile to plan.*

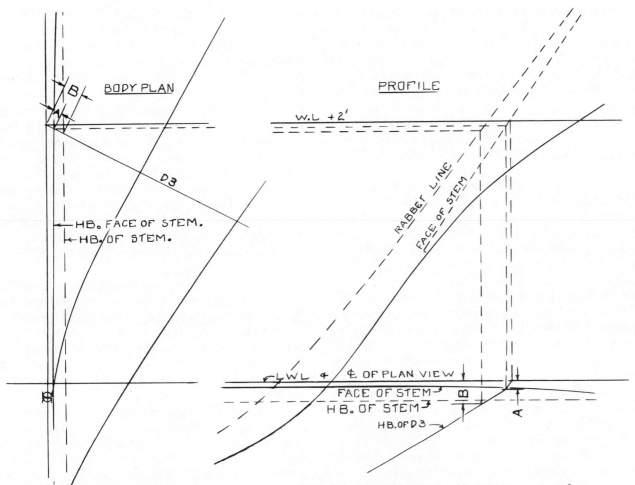

Figure 5-16. *The proper way to establish the ends of the diagonals is to project each slash distance through the stem out to the stem in profile and down to the stem in plan view.*

of -4' and stations 14 and 20 and perhaps from WL +1' on the centerline to the junctures of WL -2' with stations 14 and 20.

Sometimes the location of the unfair area makes it more appropriate to use waterlines and buttocks as checks instead of diagonals. If this is the case, don't hesitate to add them in. As you will see later on, these lines are also added to more completely define areas where the shape is changing rapidly, as in the flaring bow so popular on large motor yachts. Nothing could be more useful to the builder of such a shape than to have a grid of closely spaced waterlines and buttocks from which to pick up and form it.

I have never heard other loftsmen advocate any sequence or order in which long lines are best drawn, but I have fallen into the habit of drawing those that are most normal to the skin first. This leads to less wholesale correction, as it is relatively simple to see whether an easy curve like a diagonal or a relatively straight line like an aft buttock is fair, whereas a forward buttock or waterline under the counter can be out quite a bit and still look plausible. I have seen loftsmen start with the LWL and work both ways. Others start with the uppermost waterline and work down through them all, then run all of the buttocks, leaving the diagonals until last. Some even skip the diagonals, thinking, perhaps, that these lines have something to do with design, but not with the building.

What comes first is no big thing, and I am certainly not trying to sell my personal preferences here, but if I were lofting *Araminta*, I would probably draw the diagonals first, then the upper three and lower two waterlines, the aft buttocks, the forward part of the rest of the waterlines, and then whatever was left, in roughly that order. Some time is saved in such a sequence in that you are drawing the same types of lines in groups, so that you are not continually reaching for battens of a different size or stiffness. However, the biggest differences in the time it takes you to run the long lines and fair up the hull are not necessarily related to the sequence in which you draw the lines, but lie in the accuracy of what has been done before. The fairness and accuracy of what the designer gives you, the accuracy of the grid, the accuracy of your profile and body plan—these are what really determine how much time must be spent fairing the lines. When the above are all good and true, you can sail through the long lines so easily that you will almost feel guilty of not finding enough fairing to do.

As you draw the long lines, or at any time afterward, you can get a good idea of their fairness by "checking the crossings." Every crossing of a buttock and a waterline in the profile or plan view should be directly above or below its counterpart in the other view. That is, the intersection should be exactly the same distance forward or aft of the nearest station line. If it isn't, something is wrong. With over 30 such crossings in *Araminta*'s lines plan staring you in the face, this is a quick and easy way to assess the accuracy of the job.

Once the hull is faired, you can be concerned with details. You can fuss with the curves at the lower end of the sections under the forefoot and those along the lower edges of the keel, and you can complete any undrawn portions of the rabbet line in all three views, adjusting it as necessary to fit the faired lines. When the rabbet is faired in the profile drawing, you can draw the bearding line. The bearding line is the intersection of the back of the planking with the side of a backbone member. Its position is best figured out by making a "fid," or sample piece of planking, and placing it against the inside of each station line in the body plan where it intersects the structural member in question. With its carefully squared end placed at the rabbet line just as it would fit into the backbone member, you can mark in the bearding line against the back edge of the planking pattern.

The bearding line doesn't always appear as a separate line in the lofting; it sometimes coincides with the line that defines the

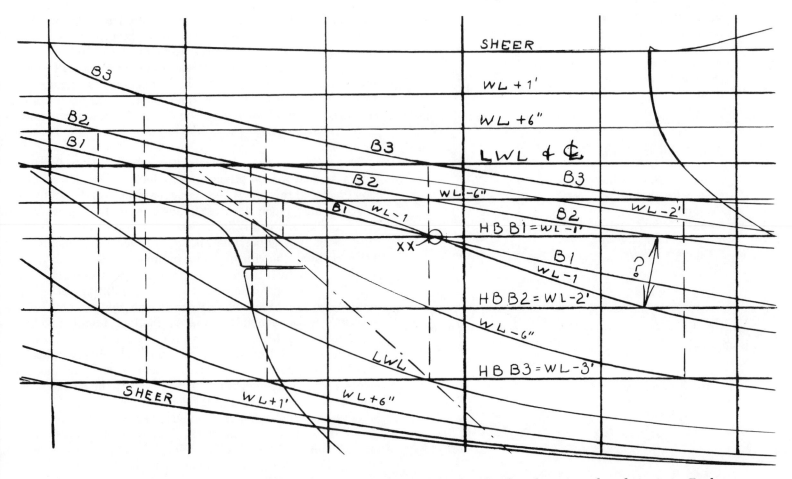

Figure 5-17. *Checking the waterline and buttock crossings of the profile relative to the plan view. Each waterline/buttock intersection in profile should be directly above its counterpart in the plan view. This is shown above by the dotted lines. The arrow indicates a pair of crossings that don't check: either WL-1 is bulging or B2 is slack. The circle notes a double crossing.*

Right: Figure 5-18. *A fid, or sample piece of planking, being used to determine where the bearding line falls.*

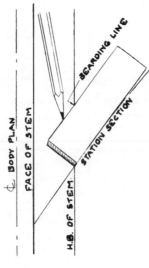

Below: Figure 5-19. *In some boats the bearding line coincides with the top of the member (right) as opposed to being separate from the edge of the member (left).*

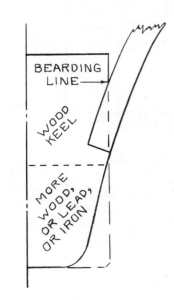

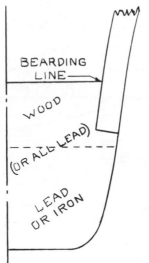

inboard face of the backbone members. In *Araminta*, the bearding line will not show separately on the keel in profile, for the planking directly intersects the keel's top face, and it will not show by itself on the stem or the horn timber in the half-breadth plan, since it is in line with the half-siding of these members. As you draw *Araminta*'s bearding line, then, you are also drawing the inboard face of some of her backbone timbers, so you may as well go on to draw the inboard faces of all the backbone members.

The third line that delineates the rabbet, the back rabbet, might be said to be optional. Many loftsmen and boatbuilders don't feel that this one is necessary, for if one has the rabbet and bearding lines and an accurate fid, he can simply chop away until the planking fits neatly in between, its lower outboard corner flush with the rabbet line and its inboard face touching the bearding line. They further point out that the back rabbet line is removed from the surface of the member as soon as one begins to cut. This is also the case where a shop has a tilting-head shaper with which to cut the rabbet. Since the only thing wanted for this operation is the angle (off normal-to-the-stem-siding) at which to tilt the cutting head, there is little need for a back rabbet. However, there are others who want the back rabbet line because it either gives them a better idea of where to head with the chisel while making guide pockets every so far along the member, or as a guide line for making a plunge cut with a Skilsaw.

While on the subject, I should discuss some features of *Araminta* that are very much involved with the rabbet. Noting that *Araminta*'s keel is rabbeted for the planking, the loftsman almost certainly will have decided that about the only practical way to put her together, using the parts as shown, would be to set up the lead keel right side up and build the boat on top of it. No doubt the next steps he would foresee would be to bolt on the fore keel and its knee, and then the rudderpost, and to set up the rest

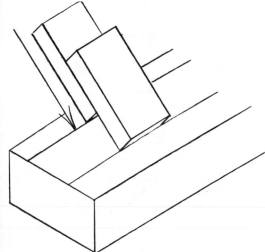

Figure 5-20. *The use of two fids of planking thickness to find the angle for cutting the rabbet.*

Figure 5-21. *The back rabbet is removed from the surface of the stem when the rabbet is cut. Where the rabbet is chopped away, a fid can be used as a guide to cutting the proper notch. With a tilting head shaper, the head is simply set at the proper angle and depth.*

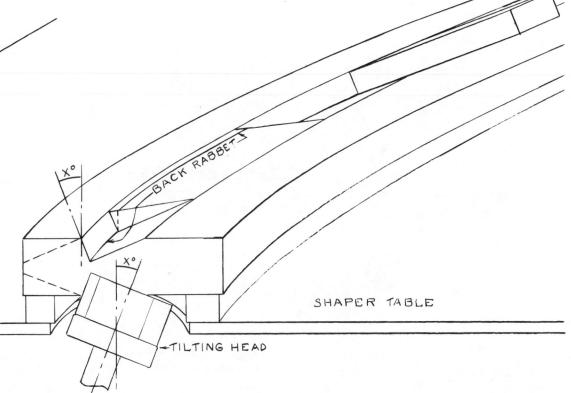

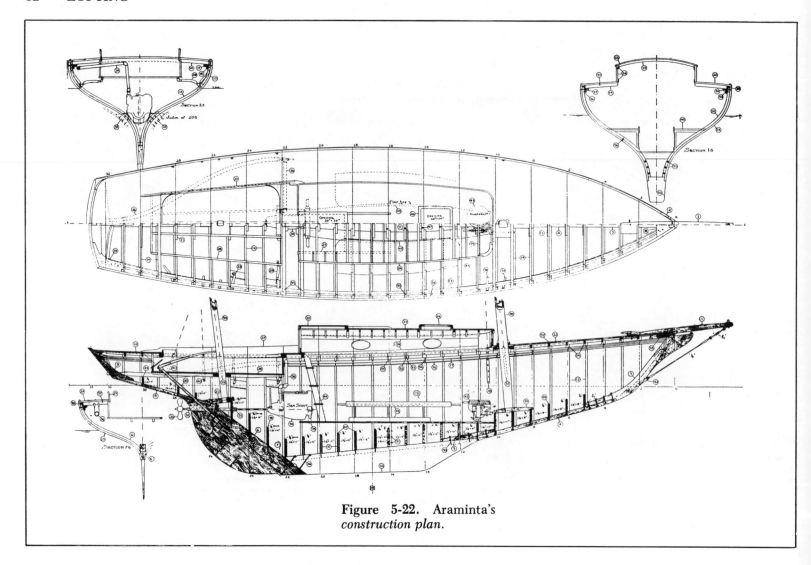

Figure 5-22. Araminta's *construction plan.*

of the backbone, including the transom. On top of this assembly would come the station moulds, but here there is a problem. All of the stations in the lines plan, which are the easiest places to pick up moulds in the body plan, are also on frame stations in the construction plan. This means that if the moulds are placed on the side of the line toward the ends of the boat they will conflict with a steam-bent frame. Here the loftsman might say to himself, "I could bend the frames around the moulds, band them to the moulds, bolt the floors to their heels, and then set up the whole assembly and lag it to the keel." That way, the boat would be half framed when set up. I believe from a picture I saw in *The Rudder* that the original *Araminta* was built that way, with the frames fitting squarely against the floors and beveled on their outboard faces to fit the planking. Carried to perfection, it would call for a mould at every frame; that is how hulls (with wooden keels) were mass produced, upside down, at the Herreshoff Manufacturing Company.

On the other hand, if our loftsman doesn't expect to build another *Araminta*, he might decide that he would prefer to install all of the floors on the backbone before putting up any moulds. This way he is working in the open, which is quicker and also easier on the knuckles. In this case, he can loft the moulds to fit on top of the floors, where they will be temporarily cleated, and then use the more conventional method of bending the ribs into a basket of ribbands on the moulds.

Both of the above procedures call for lofting the floors, for in boats of this type, I have always found that such members can be more quickly and accurately fitted when lofted and prefabricated. Where and how to pick up floors depends upon their number, location, and spacing, but with a little forethought, the job can be simplified. In this case, you can avoid the confusion of the many overlapping outlines that you would have in the body plan by drawing each floor as a half-floor

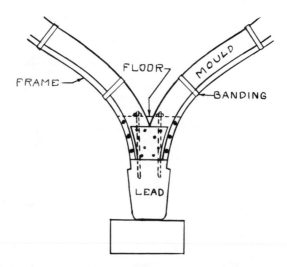

Above: Figure 5-23. *A mould setup, with the frame banded to the outside of the mould and set alongside the floor timber.* Below: Figure 5-24. *A mould setup, with the mould set atop the floors and the frames alongside. The frames are bent inside the ribbands.*

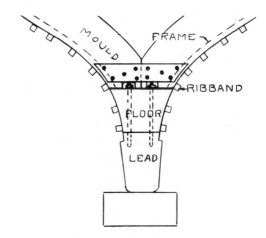

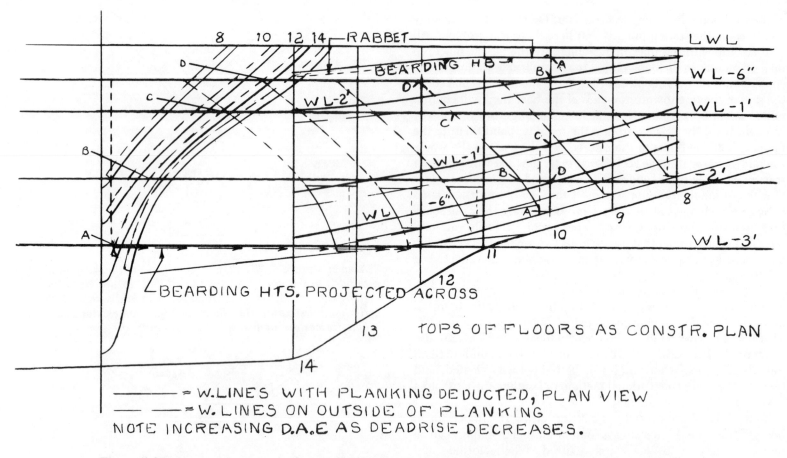

Figure 5-25. *Some of Araminta's floors fully lofted. The offsets are taken from the plan view; by using half-breadth waterlines, the measurements can be obtained for floors that lie on half-stations as well as those that lie on stations. However, the deductions are made first in the body plan and are then transferred to the half-breadth plan.*

against its own station line in the profile plan, using the station line as the centerline. You can avoid a duplication of effort by making the deductions for the planking in your body plan before picking up the offsets for the floors and drawing them directly to the inside of the planking, rather than making a deduction on each. (For an explanation of deducting for the planking, see page 43.) Third, you can establish the deducted offsets for the floors at the half stations from waterlines drawn to the inside of the planking in the plan view.

Why can't you simply make your deductions in the body plan and pick up the floors there? Wouldn't that be the simplest and least confusing method? It would be if all of *Araminta*'s floors were represented in the body plan, but there are many floors that fall in between and the body plan sections.

In *Araminta*, 20 of the 24 floors would be well defined by waterlines –6″ to –3′, inclusive, and you could draw them fairly rapidly with the following procedure:

1. Put in the station lines (these would be half stations in *Araminta*) for the intermediate floors in the profile and plan views only.
2. Draw the inside of the planking in the body plan on the regular stations. (I will explain the reason for this intermediate step in a moment.)
3. Pick up waterlines –6″ through –3′ to the inside of the planking and run these in the plan view.
4. Draw each floor, using these waterlines and the bearding line, in whichever view they appear, to get its offsets.

Draw the remaining floors from whichever long lines you choose to the *outside* of the planking, and deduct for the planking on the spot, if half-station floors, but draw them right in the body plan if on stations (or take deducted offsets to the station in profile if you prefer).

Note that you made the planking deductions for the waterlines on the body plan sections and then transferred the deducted waterlines to the plan view, instead of taking the seemingly easier step of making the deductions on the plan view waterlines in the first place. The deductions made this way will be more accurate than if you used the simpler method, for as a whole, the section lines are more normal to the plane of the planking than are the waterlines. Though *Araminta*'s lower waterlines are fairly normal to the sections, the higher or more oblique waterlines would yield an inaccurate deduction if you simply paralleled them in the plan view at the thickness of the planking, and the floors would not fit with the moulds picked up in the body plan.

In a boat with wide, flat floors, you might choose to use buttock lines rather than waterlines, perhaps putting in a few extra buttocks to get enough points, but the rest of the procedure would go the same as above. I have also lofted many sets of floors with a special set of diagonals placed to subtend them most conveniently. However, when you use buttock or diagonal offsets at each station along the profile, it means that you have to set up the body plan grid-form view of these lines at each and every station, which should bring a groan from even the most patient soul. But, in the case of diagonals, this can be greatly simplified by building a simple trap or spider web of straightedge sticks over the body plan with which you can quickly rule in the needed lines at any station. And where buttocks are used, temporary frame-spaced buttocks can be drawn in as shown in Figure 5-27 to facilitate the job.

Having determined the face of the floor at the station line, you must now determine the floor's bevels. The bevel of the bottom of a floor, where it fits on a backbone member, is, of course, the angle of the station line with the member right there where you have drawn the floor.

The bevel of the side of a floor where it fits against the planking

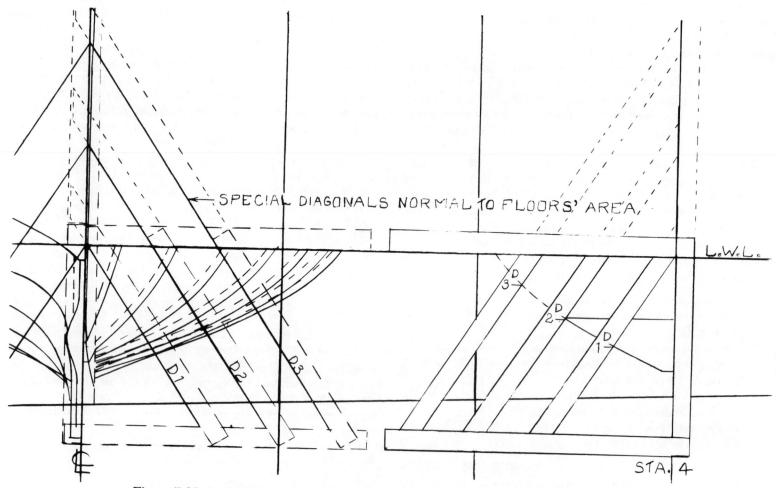

Figure 5-26. *Special diagonals set up for picking up the floors' measurements on a boat with moderate or little deadrise. A portable rack corresponding to the grid of the special diagonals hastens the process.*

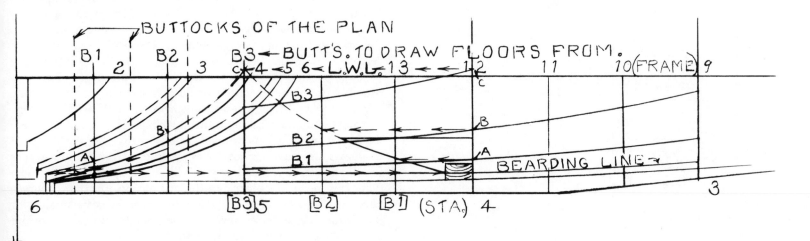

Figure 5-27. *Lofting the floors by the use of buttocks. Frame-spaced buttocks reduce confusion, allowing the use of existing station lines. The buttocks of the plan are ignored here.*

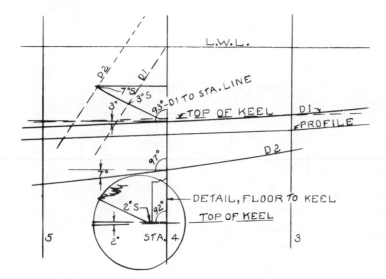

Figure 5-28. *The bevels of a floor being taken from half-breadth diagonals. The angle between the diagonal and the station line is picked up and applied to the station drawing of the floor where the diagonal intersects it. The bevel for the base is simply measured in the profile as the angle between the top of the keel and the vertical.*

usually changes slightly from bottom to top; on a tall floor it can change quite a bit. As can readily be seen in the lines plan, bevels taken on waterline –3′ and on the bearding line in the plan view would be reasonably good, for these lines are close to normal to the section lines of the floors along the lead keel. However, remember that such bevels are only true in the plane of the angle with the beveled surface at which they were picked up. Since you usually saw the bevel with a blade that is cutting normal to the edge of the wood, any bevels taken at an angle with the edge become less and less useful as the angle increases. But if you have used the method mentioned above where several special diagonals are drawn as normal as possible to those sections where the floors will be picked up, you will now reap a big bonus. The diagonals' perpendicularity to the sections assures that accurate bevels can be picked right off the crossings of these diagonals with the station lines in the plan view and assigned to the same crossing of each diagonal with each floor in the half section.

When such is not the case, you can make the best of it by lifting all the bevels you need from the body plan, which is done in the following manner:

1. Set up three short station lines with standard spacing and a horizontal line running through them, or pick a place where this situation already exists that is relatively clear of other drawings, such as at stations 0, 2, and 4, where WL –2′ runs through them.

2. Place a rule or pickup stick across and normal to the station in the body plan at which you want to take the bevel and at the point where you want the bevel; then measure or mark off the distance to each of the adjacent stations.

3. Take these two offsets into the "situation" established in step 1. The three short station lines represent the three that you measured in the body plan, and they are in the same fore-and-aft relationship as in a bit of the plan view of

them. Mark in the offsets on the stations, setting a pick *above* the horizontal line at the offset of the station nearest the end of the boat and one *below* the line at the offset of the station toward the middle of the boat. The crossing of the horizontal line at the center station is the point where you want the bevel; a batten through this point and the other two will form the bevel. (*See* Figure 5-29.)

What you have done is to draw a short, three-station segment of a diagonal that is exactly normal to the section at the point where you want to take the bevel. One could hardly get a better bevel than that, and this is the method most commonly used to pick up the bevels of sawn frames, bulkheads, moulds, or any other transverse parts. The bevels of the floors between the stations can be found by setting up intermediate stations at the proper interval between the stations you have set up. This can be done well enough to avoid the labor of drawing and measuring these separately in the body plan. In a sawn-frame vessel, however, you would probably draw all of the frames, either in the body plan or on a scrive board.

When there are many bevels to pick up, it is worth the trouble to drill and pin the batten so that it pivots on the center station, and then tack down a plastic protractor, or even make up the whole business as a portable "bevel finder" on a loose piece of plywood and drag it about the floor with you.

Remember that what you pick up will represent either the large or the small face of the floor, and that you will have to know which side you are dealing with when you come to sawing out the floor. This will be no problem if, in addition to recording the angle of the bevel, you also record whether it is a standing or an under bevel. You will then know which way to tilt the saw or saw table when cutting out the floor.

Very early in the game on *Araminta*, you will need a pattern of the lead keel. Without it, nothing can be set up, and I prefer to

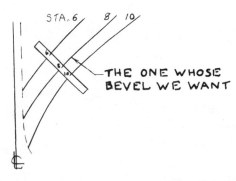

Figures **5-29** and **5-30.** *A quick method of establishing short sections for taking bevels. Measurements to the body plan sections (Figure 5-29) adjacent to the section where the bevel is wanted yield offsets that can be used to draw a short diagonal in the half-breadth view of the situation. The short diagonal is drawn through the offsets, which are applied to a three-station grid in the manner shown below. Bevels for floors between the body plan sections can be found by dropping intermediate stations into the grid.*

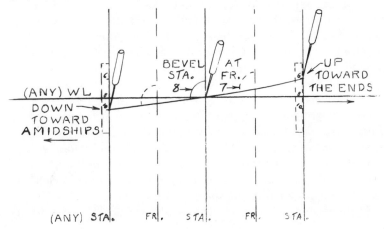

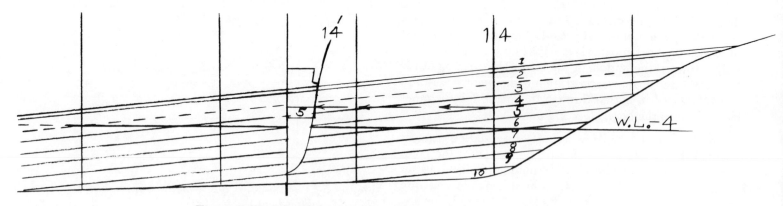

Figure 5-31. *A keel pattern of 2-inch lifts oriented parallel to the rabbet line. The half-breadth of a lift is taken where its top face (the widest face) intersects a station.*

put this item ahead of others in the sequence listed at the beginning of this chapter so that the lead keel will have been cast before you finish the lofting. What sort of pattern, or patterns, you make will depend on how you chose to pour the keel. If a regular foundry does it, you may be asked for a one-piece pattern or model of the keel. A simple way to do this would be to assemble lifts of solid wood similar to those used in a waterline-lift model boat. However, after studying this keel with its rabbeted top edges and straight top, it should occur to you that the waterlines cross the rabbet at an angle and would make an intricate job of it. A series of waterlines tilted to parallel the keel's top would simplify cutting the rabbet. You should also be mindful that the thickness of the lumber available for the pattern's construction should be considered in the spacing of these lines.

A professional foundry might cast this particular keel with a removable CO_2-treated sand core made around the rabbet of the pattern, but if the keel is to be cast in an open-top sand mold, you can make a wood pattern of the keel up to the rabbet line only and then make a weighted split core that will sit on top of the sand and form the rabbet. For fiberglass construction, the rabbet line is eliminated altogether, as the keel will either be dropped into the hull or bolted to a flush outside surface. Should you be lofting *Araminta* as a production boat in fiberglass, your job then would be to make stations and templates to be used to weld up a steel mold into which keels could be repeatedly cast.

Whatever the casting system, lead always shrinks as it cools, and to get the correct size keel, you must always build patterns and molds proportionately large all over. Although different casting methods can result in different shrinkages, a ⅛-inch-to-the-foot shrinkage allowance has always worked just fine for the

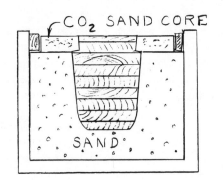
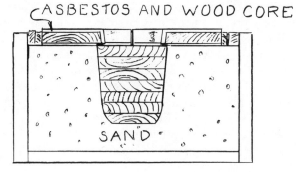

Figure 5-32. *Cross-sections of two sand molds, showing two methods of forming the rabbet. The one on the left requires a full pattern, while the one on the right requires a pattern to the rabbet only.*

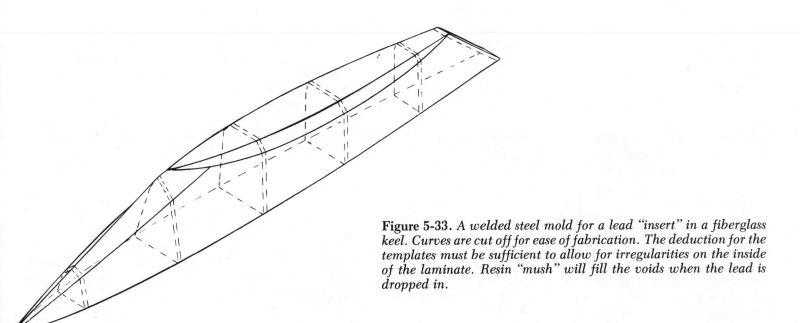

Figure 5-33. *A welded steel mold for a lead "insert" in a fiberglass keel. Curves are cut off for ease of fabrication. The deduction for the templates must be sufficient to allow for irregularities on the inside of the laminate. Resin "mush" will fill the voids when the lead is dropped in.*

simple sand and steel molds I have used. Professional pattern makers make their measurements on the pattern with a "shrinkage rule" (where each foot is stretched by varying amounts), which you could easily make up. However, since *Araminta*'s keel is but a foot wide and less than 2 feet tall, you have only to stretch each 2-foot station spacing ¼", add a tiny fraction (the adjustments' exact dimensions depend on the lifts' thicknesses) to each lift, and add not over 1/16" to each half-breadth to get a keel that's "right on."*

Once the keel pattern has gone to the foundry, you can concentrate on making patterns of all of the backbone members, half-patterns of all the floors, the transom rack and the transom half-pattern, and then the moulds, in about that order. Such a sequence should keep the people on the floor supplied with parts that they can use as fast as they get them, meaning that nothing will have to be put aside while waiting for something else to be made ready. But you should allow some lead time for lofting; on a boat like *Araminta* it could easily be three weeks before there is enough work ahead to keep a boatbuilder or two continuously busy from then on.

Before getting into the transom, you should draw and make up a deck crown pattern or a deck beam pattern. That there is a difference between the two should be obvious, since the crown is the shape of the top of the decking, while the beam pattern consists of, technically, two curves parallel to the crown and "tucked inside" it. This difference only has significance in regard to the two

---

*An exception to this rule occurs when you are casting a very tall keel. Due to the tremendous pressure of the lead bearing down on the sand, you can forget about allowing for shrinkage in the heights, and you will also have to vigorously pound sand at the bottom of the mold to prevent the keel from compressing the sand too much.

edges of the deck beam on a severely curved deck. If you forget that the two curves should be parallel—the bottom one should be slightly smaller than the top one—and use the same curve for both edges, then the deck beam will thin out toward the ends. To see why this happens you have only to superimpose two circles of the same diameter, one slightly above the other. At some point the two circles will cross one another and the area in between the tops of the two circles will thin out as you move toward the circles' edges. On a highly crowned deck, such convergence of the deck beam edges can cause difficulties, such as when notching the beam into a certain height of clamp, and when fitting a certain thickness of insulation between the top and underside of the deck. In flat crowns, such as are found on most main decks, the curves are such short segments of such wide circles that deck beams cut using the same curve will not be noticeably deeper in the middle than at the ends. Thus, in most cases, builders, if not loftsmen, simply make one curve and use it for everything. As long as you keep the difference straight for the occasional case where the difference is critical, why not use this shortcut?

The drawing of the crown usually comes as a pleasant change of pace at the end of drawing all the sections in the body plan, where you need it to draw the top of the transom's half-section. Some designers include a drawing that shows how they expect the crown to be developed, as there are several favorite shapes, or sometimes a special shape is called for by the designer. Others are satisfied with the arc of a long radius, which at least has the virtue that all members associated with any part of the deck have the same curves. Still others are so concerned with the profile of the deck, or house, that they require you to vary the crown all the way along to fit between the centerline and the outboard edge in profile. *Araminta*'s designer seems to have used radii. What he says is, "Crown of deck ⅜" to 1', or 3⅜" in 9'," and nothing about the house top, which seems to be about a 6'6" radius. Who could blame him if he said, "Why should I write down every little thing when the builder has a rule? Besides, the owner may want the house raised to clear his wife's head anyway."

Of course, the number of possible deck crown shapes is unlimited, as is the number of ways to draw them. With fiberglass construction, hard curves can be fabricated as easily as the flatter ones long associated with wood and metal, and they tend to add a stiffness to fiberglass that that material lacks. The possibilities offered by fiberglass have really taken the lid off in this design area. A few of the traditional methods of developing a crown were shown in Chapter 2, but for turtlebacks, gullwings, and football-like cambered decks, you are on your own when the designer doesn't spell it out for you.

The pleasure of developing the transom for *Araminta* has been preempted by Mr. Herreshoff, which is just as well, because I want to save this subject for a separate chapter. (*See* Chapter 9) However, you still have to draw the development full size and make a half (or full) pattern for use in building it. Also, though you may note in the construction plan that the hull and transom meet in a mitered seam, you will have to pick up bevels for the border or fashion pieces (to which the hood ends of the planking are screwed). With so many buttocks and half-buttocks, it is best to pick up the bevels along these, and then perhaps run a few short waterlines in the topsides. Because of its rake and curvature, *Araminta*'s transom is not the easiest to get the bevels for; it would be considerably easier if the transom were plumb and flat.

You will want to divide the angle of transom to hull planking more or less evenly, otherwise, one of the two edges will be feathered too much to be able to withstand caulking. This comes about naturally when the transom and the side planking are about the same thickness, as on *Araminta*. But if one planking face were much thicker than the other, you might want to rabbet it to avoid feathering the thinner planking. What you have to do on this boat

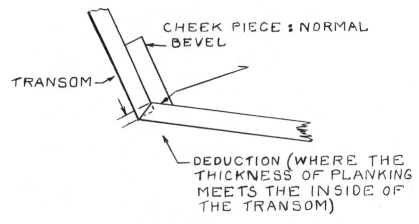

Figure 5-34. *A mitered transom seam.*

is simply to make the transom full size on the outside, bevel it under to the line of the thickness of the side planking deducted on the inboard side, and then fit the fashion pieces to this line. The fashion pieces must have a bevel to fit the inside of the planking, which means that the transom assembly will have a double set of bevels.

Another job for the loftsman and/or the boatbuilder—they often are the same person—is to lay out a rack on which the transom can be bent and assembled. This would have the 9-foot radius given, less the thickness of the transom planking, and also less the thickness of the fashion pieces if they are to be made up and put down first.

Another good thing to do while in the transom area would be to make up the "stern beam" with its two lodging knees, which all fit against the transom. Although many builders saw out the beam part extra wide (or laminate or steam bend it) and scribe it into place after whacking out a couple of extra-thick knees, it saves time if you loft these parts and fit them to the transom, perhaps leaving

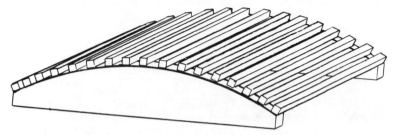

Figure 5-35. *A rack for bending and assembling the transom.*

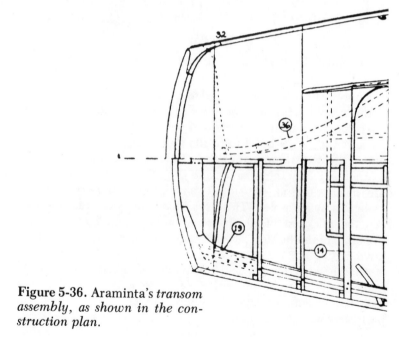

Figure 5-36. Araminta's *transom assembly, as shown in the construction plan.*

a little excess wood on the forward ends of the knees until after frame 31 and the clamp and shelf are in place. When these pieces are "gotten out" *on* the boat by any but the most skillful builders, the results can be awful; the builder who prefabricates them, fits them, and lays them aside (heavily coated with red lead) is really ahead. Looking at it in the plane of the deck, this assembly will have the crown of the deck beam crown pattern; looking down on it, its outboard edges will have the outline of the stern in the plan view, less the apparent thickness of the transom and hull planking in that view. It will also have the bevels of the transom and sheer strake. Thus, fitting the transom can be quite difficult, and while lofting won't make the job itself less demanding, it can save you from a lot of frustration.

There is not too much to say about the patterns of the other backbone members. You will want patterns in profile of all of these, complete with pertinent details, such as scarfs, joints, the rabbet line, the bearding line if it shows, a station line for every frame, bolt locations, the propeller shaft, the rudder stock, gudgeon locations, and some waterlines with which to keep things on the level. If this seems to be an overly long list, think twice. It's a better bet that you have missed some items whose locations you can never get as accurately if you must measure for them later inside the boat than if you simply draw them in now.

For some members, especially those whose sided dimensions are not constant, you will need a plan view pattern too, unless you want to lay out this view on the stock. Many times it is quicker to pick up offsets and pursue the latter method, because patterns of the inboard or outboard faces of such members cannot be lifted directly anywhere but on a level surface, and *Araminta*, for instance, has none that are level. Your choice of methods here might well hinge on whether there is to be more than one boat built to this plan, but a good pattern is often a worthwhile investment, particularly if others are going to grab your work and run, leaving you with doubts that you will be around to lay out the missing information at the critical moment.

Don't forget to draw a pattern of the rudder with plenty of pertinent detail on it.

"There!" you mutter to yourself, having gotten grumpy, stiff kneed, and a little fatter—lofting's occupational hazards. "Maybe that'll keep them [the boatbuilders] busy while I get out the moulds."

Picking up the moulds can be a welcome burst of activity after lofting a boat of any complexity, and perhaps that is why it usually gets done very quickly. Given some clear stock (usually plywood today), a small band saw, and some fastenings (screws are best), it is fun to see the stack of moulds grow. So much so that you are likely to lose your head and forget some of the markings and other useful details that every mould needs.

Some of the things to remember about the moulds you would make for *Araminta* are as follows:

- Since there will be a steam-bent frame beside each mould (if you go the route of setting each mould atop a floor), all butt blocks, or "scabs," and braces are best kept off the face toward the end of the boat.
- The moulds will need vertical cleats, possibly notched, to attach them to the floors and align them with the station line.
- There will have to be notches in the bottoms of the moulds for the keel bolts.
- If the builder decides to place a mould at every two-foot station, they can be relatively lightly built.

For round-bottomed hull moulds in general the following advice is offered:

- It is worthwhile to keep the center post of all moulds on the same side of the centerline so you can tell at a glance whether the moulds line up. Also, you can then run a flat board with a straight edge against these posts over the tops of the sheer cross spalls. The tops of the cross spalls should be placed at the sheer so that you always know where it is.
- You should be careful that the sheer marked on the mould is the sheer height as squared over from the line at the outside of the planking, not the intersection of the mould's line with the sheerline that caps the body plan. That particular height is utterly meaningless. I once got an awful start when I tried to put a batten on a set of sheer marks that had been picked up just that way. What a mess it was until I found out what was wrong.
- You should try to assemble the moulds so that they are simple, clean, and offer the least obstruction to climbing around in the boat that can be managed without weakening the setup.

Since there are so many other topics to cover, we must move on. Hopefully, this chapter has shed light on some of the facets of lofting a round-bottomed boat. The various lines and the moves made in lofting them are so interrelated that every procedure learned tends to contribute to a better understanding of other parts of the process. This is to say that as you go deeper into lofting, the moves familiar to you become levers with which you can work out other procedures. Therefore, you needn't worry yet about not understanding everything. The more you loft the clearer it seems, and the more fascinating it becomes.

6 / Minimum Lofting a Round-Bottomed Auxiliary Sailboat

If you would like to plunge into building a round-bottomed boat lofting only those components that are absolutely essential, you will only need to loft the following items, not necessarily in the order given:

- *The Body Plan.* Draw the station sections, deduct the planking thickness, and pick up the moulds.
- *The Backbone in Profile.* This can be done in segments if a full-size loft floor is not available. Mark off the rabbet line from the plan and the table of offsets. Draw the bearding line (and the back rabbet if wanted) from the offsets established by the planking deductions on the sections. The latter two will be quite accurate on the more horizontal members but less so on the stem and rudderpost. When in doubt, leave the chopping until the boat is set up. Pick up profile patterns of the members, which should be well marked with station and waterlines to aid setting up.
- *The Lead Keel.* From procedures 1 and 2 above, make up patterns or actual parts for the lead keel casting pattern or pick up information for building a direct mold. Remember to add on for shrinkage in either case.

You should now build the boat, getting all information from the plans and "off the boat" for setting up and making parts not present in the minimum lofting. At the same time, it is well to remember that you need only be limited to the above amount of lofting if you want to be, and that if anything bothers you, you need only employ a bit of abbreviated lofting such as is described in Chapter 4 to sort things out. Sometimes drawing even a single line will save a lot of milling around.

On the other hand, some parts need no lofting whatsoever. Take *Araminta*'s trailboards, for instance. Obviously it is possible to loft and pick up the information for chopping them out or to build a pair of racks with the port and starboard twist for laminating them. However, don't forget that the planked-up hull can serve as a rack on which the trailboards can be made and glued up in place. Since trailboards so made couldn't fit better, no lofting is needed to get these parts.

In a construction like *Araminta*'s, you should pick up those floors that fall on a station, make them, and lag them to the lead keel. In the last chapter I showed how to pick up the bevels of these floors in the body plan. The shape of the intermediate floors would be a guess without further lofting, but you can run some ribbands on the installed floors and then fit the intermediates and install them too. To get the intermediate floors that are bolted and drifted high on the stem and after members, it is easiest if you work from the middle of the boat toward both ends, setting up moulds as preceding floors are installed. Then put on the actual ribbands to which the ribs will be bent and fit the next floors to these.

In designs where the floor spacing does not coincide with the sections used for moulds, the way of getting floors early in the setup without lofting them would be to set up the moulds and put on enough ribbands to give you the shape of the floors. Again, you should work from the middle toward the ends to minimize reaching and climbing into the ribbanded frame.

When there is no rabbeted keel like *Araminta*'s, you can leave any or all floors out of the boat as long as you wish—many boats have been built this way. A builder may wish to laminate the floors in place, take patterns for some special metal floors from the inside of the skin, or even land floors atop the frames. But there eventually comes a day of reckoning when it takes much longer to fit and fasten a floor than it would to either loft it or fit it early in the game—which is something to ponder with every part of a boat.

Even a curved, raked transom can be fitted in place on a boat without expanded drawings and patterns or much special lofting. This was frequently done in the past by the less sophisticated boatbuilders, but today it is used even by professionals when what is being set up is a simple framework for a one-off fiberglass boat or a plug for fiberglass tooling. Since we will get into these "disposable" structures in the chapter on one-offs and tooling, it suffices to say that the methods used to mock up transoms on them are similar to what you can do on an actual boat. Three basic procedures are these:

1. Make up an oversize transom, set it up in place, and trim it to fit, using fairing battens laid across the moulds forward of it.

2. Carry the hull lines to a fairing station abaft the transom (sometimes the designer has already done this), build and set up a mould at this station, and then fit the fashion pieces, a pattern of the transom, or even the transom itself, at its proper location within the basket of ribbands running to the fairing station. Saw off everything past the transom.

3. Make a rack or form of stringers representing buttock lines and transom radius lines, drawing extra buttocks into the lines plan as needed to cover the transom well; then set up the form at its proper location and rake, run ribbands to the buttock line stringers, and build the transom on the form.

Procedure 1 is best used for simple transoms and boats with a simply shaped afterbody.

Procedure 2 is possible with almost any type of boat or transom, but with all the stringers converging, it can be a tight place to work on boats with narrow sterns. There is no question, however, that this method will keep the hull's lines perfectly accurate right to the transom.

Procedure 3 is a method I worked out when a set of moulds but no trace of a transom, either physically or as lofting, was brought to me for the building of a one-off fiberglass hull. I had been told that everything needed to set her up was there, and under the circumstances it didn't seem diplomatic to announce to the owner that he would have to pay for several days of lofting the stern; so I built the transom in place. As this was one of those curved, raked, elliptical transoms that fairs into a counter with a lot of tumblehome, I felt that I had really gotten away with something.

Building a transom using one of the shortcuts outlined above can have its pitfalls, however. Years ago, we cold-molded a curved transom in my shop and fitted it directly—scribing it down in place and trimming it to size—to a racing sailboat hull, which had been cold-molded with its counter left open at the designed reverse rake. Perhaps the transom was not carefully enough centered, leveled, or horned before it was scribed down in place. Whatever the case was, something went wrong and the stern was just a touch lopsided. That didn't affect the boat's good racing record, but it did hurt my pride. After that, it was back to the loft for transoms. So be careful!

Lofting a V-bottomed boat is somewhat of a cross—in varying degrees—between lofting the flat-bottomed and round-bottomed types that we have discussed already. The presence of a chine means that the extensive curves found in round-bottomed hulls will be absent; yet the V-bottomed configuration allows for arced sections. Possible hull forms range from vessels having simple straight-line sections to deep-V powerboats that are neither slab-sided nor slab-bottomed. For the loftsman, the former would be child's play to loft, while the latter would have enough curves, "lift strips," and other details to hold a loftsman's interest. As my purpose in writing this book is to teach the reader as much as possible about various lofting techniques, I have chosen one of the deep-V hulls designed by C. Raymond Hunt Associates to illustrate this chapter.

When Ray Hunt developed the deep-V bottom, he made an important breakthrough in the art of high-speed powerboat design. His continuation of a relatively steep deadrise right to the stern, with the bottom of the V rounded off from station 4 or 5 (of a 10-station waterline design) aft, gave us an excellent bottom shape for crashing into seas at high speed. This has been well proven by the number of boats of this type that have been consistent winners in rough water powerboat races for the last 20 years.

As you study the lines of this 36-foot fast cruiser you cannot help but admire them. The sheer exudes speed and power as it rises forward to accentuate the stem's aggressive rake. It slopes aft with but a few inches of sweep in its length, never quite leveling off; yet it seems to turn and lift at the stern due to the generous crown of the taffrail. The bow profile from keel to deck is one flowing line that is pleasing to look at afloat or ashore, and the sharply curved, raked transom is a neat treatment of a "barn door" situation.

If I seem to have gone overboard in my enthusiasm, perhaps I should explain that I was involved in building over a dozen deep-V vessels from 12 to 48 feet off and on for almost 20 years. The early models, while functional, had not attained this degree of harmony in their lines. It takes time and many individual designs to refine any type of boat aesthetically—this boat was drawn more than 10 years after the first one. This is how a "classic" is created, and although they may not realize it, loftsmen have a front row seat in observing such developments.

Just as the rail and the "bottom at side" control the shape of a flat-bottomed skiff or sharpie, so do the sheer, chine, and keel profile dominate the shape of a V-bottomed boat. There's a lot that can be changed between these three lines, but they still establish the boat's length, beam, draft, rough displacement, and range of performance possibilities. Obviously the chine is as important as the other two lines in establishing the basic characteristics of the hull. Therefore, the chine is a sort of third dimension that is always included when you draw and fair the profile and sheer before going on to the other lines. When these

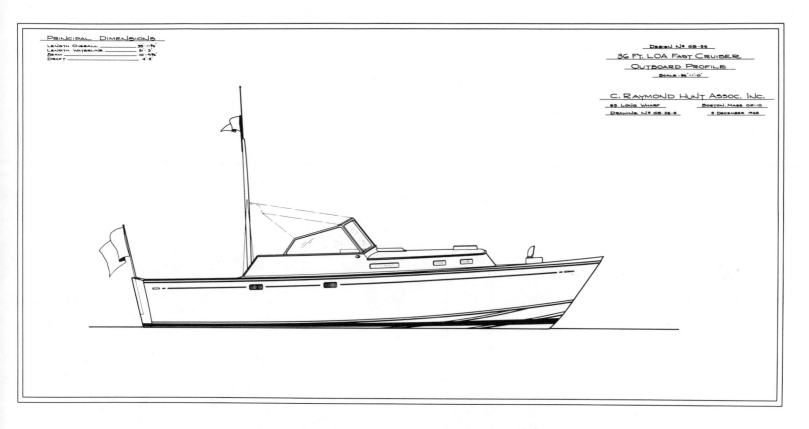

Figure 7-1. *Outboard profile of the 36-foot Hunt powerboat.*

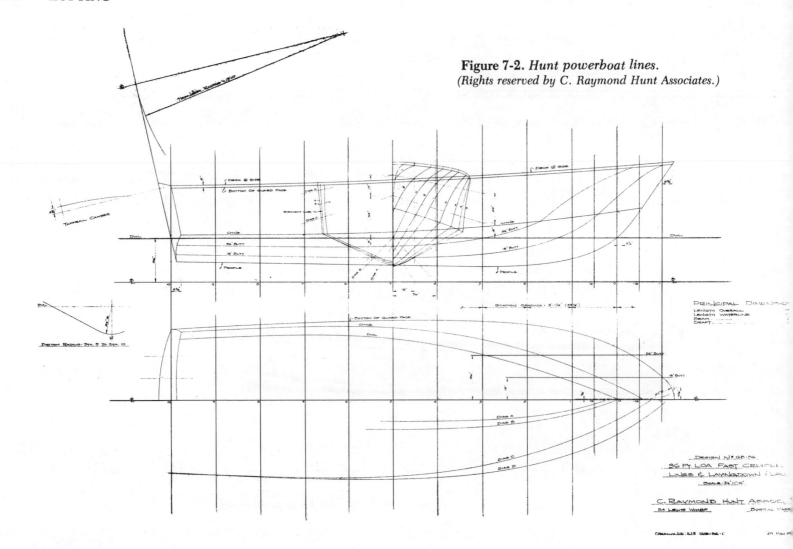

Figure 7-2. *Hunt powerboat lines.*
(*Rights reserved by C. Raymond Hunt Associates.*)

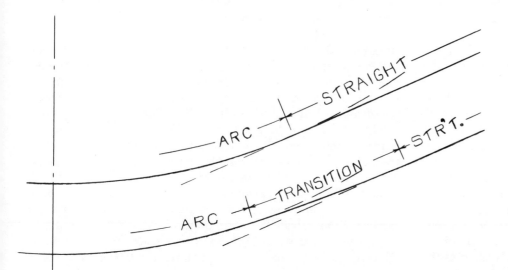

Figure 7-3. *A straight-line section faired into an arced keel area.*

three lines are done in both profile and plan views, you are a long way into the lofting of a V-bottomed boat.

Once the sheer, chine, and profile are drawn and faired in the profile and half-breadth plans, you can move on to the body plan. Here you will find that aft of station 5 each section from the chine down is a straight line that is tangent to the 24-inch-radius arc that forms the rounded keel area. In practice, it has been found that the sudden transition from straight line to arc is likely to produce an apparent ridge or knuckle in the bottom. A smoother transition and a less mechanical look result if you swing the bottom line out until it is about ¼″ away from tangency, and then fair the arc from near that point out to blend with the deadrise. (*See* Figure 7–3.)

Forward of station 5 the 2-foot radius of the bottom sharpens until it has only a ⅜″ radius in the forefoot as it swings up to the chine. From here the radius increases again until at the deck it is

20 inches. To guide you in fairing the deck and any other long lines you might use at the bow, a fairing or ghost line is shown in the body and half-breadth plans, with an indication at the deck of how to fair the long lines to it and sweep in a radius. The shape of this flaring conical nose is best worked out on the floor and then reworked and literally carved to its final shape on the boat, for its looks are extremely sensitive to slight changes in the area where the long lines and the radii blend. To fair this area on the floor, indeed to construct it, you should add in a grid of short waterlines running back to station ½; this gives you a closely spaced definition of its shape. You should cross these with some closely spaced buttock lines to check on the flow of the shape down along the stem. When this lofting takes three-dimensional form in the boat, it will need close attention—and maybe even a little plastic surgery—if you are to capture its elusive good looks.

This boat's plans show only two buttocks and four diagonals for fairing those parts of the sections not controlled by the sheer, chine, and profile at centerline—many fewer long lines than a round-bottomed boat this size might have. With straighter sections there might be fewer such lines, and with absolutely straight section lines, none at all. On the other hand, as I have said so many times, nobody, least of all the designer, will be upset at any additional long lines you draw in.

While other lines are important for looks, the most important lines in high-speed powerboats are those that shape the run—the chine, buttocks, and centerline profile in the afterbody. At planing speeds the water hurtling under the bottom aft can build up tremendous positive and negative pressures; these can radically—and at times violently— affect the boat's performance. To cite but one of a complexity of factors, hooked or concave buttocks in the run tend to depress the bow, while round or convex buttocks tend to raise it. These effects become magnified as the speed increases. Therefore, you should be extremely careful to abide by the intentions of the designer in the lines of a high-speed bottom. Nor should you get huffy if the designer checks and rechecks this area or insists on what might seem to be picayune adjustments in either the lofting or in the boat as set up.

A common adjunct to deep-V hulls are the so-called "lift strips" that appear in various numbers, shapes, and sizes on different designs. These look and work like a series of extra chines grafted to the bottom. Without getting into their hydrodynamics, it is generally agreed that the effectiveness of lift strips is dependent on water breaking off the outboard edge of the bottom surfaces cleanly and not flowing up around the sides or further up the hull. Many early strips had the bottom surface angled downward and the sides undercut to ensure a clean break. In fact, an early name for similar devices was "water break." You would be well advised, therefore, to keep the corners of lift strips as clean and sharp and to keep the sides as close to vertical as possible. Yet, if you are lofting a fiberglass stock boat, you might have pressure from the production people to round the corners and give the sides more draft, since this would make their work easier. This just goes to show that loftsmen can get caught in the middle between designers and builders. In such a case, while you're waiting for the dust to settle, just make sure that the profile and half-breadth sweep of the strips is sweet and fair.

The after end or termination of a lift strip should not be extended or shortened without the approval of the designer, for the trail of broken water or bubbles from it can cause propeller cavitation. This applies equally to skegs, keel shoes, and to the location of any other appendages near the stern of a high-speed powerboat. While these may not be in line with a propeller when the boat is on a straight course, they can cause trouble in a turn when the angled stream of their disturbance finds a wheel or when the lower unit of an outboard or inboard/outboard is turned into that stream.

At this time, there are probably only four building systems for which you are likely to have to loft and set up a high-speed powerboat: cold-molded wood, aluminum, one-off in fiberglass, or as tooling for a production fiberglass hull. Until some new procedure is invented, these methods seem to combine the best physical properties and construction costs needed for a boat of this type. (When this picture changes, few people will be involved in it sooner than the loftsman, and that's another interesting facet of the trade.) With both cold-molded and foam sandwich one-offs the DAE can be rather pronounced on full powerboat bows from chine to deck due to large deductions for the thick stringers and skins likely to be used. While it involves more work, notching the stringers into the moulds simplifies making these deductions.

Since powerboat designers are especially fond of the 10-station waterline for the purpose of comparing performance and trim data in different hull sizes, you will often find that big boats of

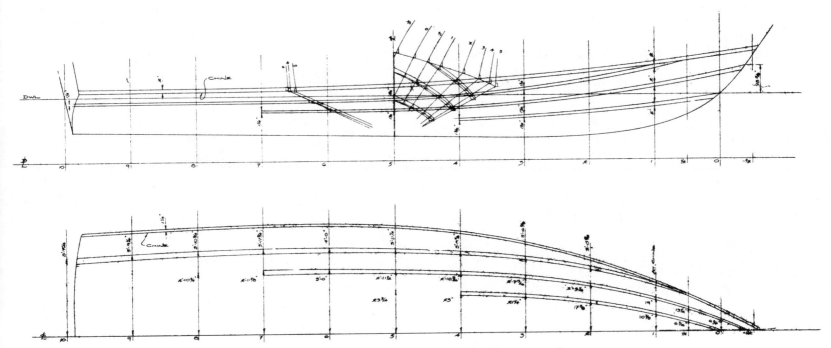

Figure 7-4. *The lift strip arrangement on the Hunt powerboat.*

this type have rather long station spaces. This calls for heavy, well-braced moulds, and heavy stringers, or intermediate moulds unless some bulkheads are included in the setup. Designers often give half stations in the curved bows, but rarely aft where the shape doesn't change much. Yet this is where you have to be particularly careful about distortion of the run, so extra stringers and moulds to stiffen the bottom aft will be well worth the trouble.

In general, powerboats are uncomplicated to loft, except for those that have bows that are difficult to fair. However, the relatively straight lines of their midbodies and afterbodies should not lull you into carelessness. The slight curves that look so simple to draw can be harder to make fair than the jaunty curves found in some classic sailboats—it's easier to spoil a subtle curve than a bold one.

It should be obvious that, all else being equal, one is more likely to get away with minimum lofting a V-bottomed boat than a round-bottomed boat, because when the three dominant lines (sheer, profile, and chine) are faired, the hull is divided into four panels whose potential trouble areas are not only limited, but bounded by fair lines to which they can be easily compared. At the same time, the three controlling lines are themselves relatively easy to fair, because they are prominences or edges of the shape that can be unmistakably eyeballed by anybody with one good eye. What I am saying is that if you put down only the body plan of a V-bottomed boat, make deductions, run a floor line, pick up moulds, and set them up with perhaps a transom frame at one end and a profiled stem at the other, your chances of getting a reasonably fair and accurate hull are good.

I am *not* saying, however, that if one has the space and the time to lay down at least the three dominant lines, that he would not be far better off for doing so. Not on your life! Not after listening to the deafening silence on the phone one afternoon when I mentioned to "Win" Willard of the Hunt office that there would be a chapter in this book on minimum lofting the V-bottomed powerboat. He might as well have shouted, "You know better than that! What do you think we draw long lines for, our health?" To put the record straight, I don't recommend that a professional omit most of the lofting of *any* boat for a client, and never, never for tooling. Certainly, I never have. But for one's

own account, for a do-it-yourselfer, why not? It's a matter of the home builder saving resources, the scarcest of which are often time and money, versus professionalism where accuracy is expected by the owner and his designer.

The conical bow on the 36-foot deep-V example would be difficult to loft any way but fully. Therefore, the best treatment for minimum lofting this boat might be either to loft it fully in the bow only at the scale of the plans, to get a grid to help in setting up, or simply to ignore everything forward of station –1 until the boat is set up, and then put up an oversize block of wood or foam, and carve out a suitable shape in place. This fudging would have to be carried as far down as station –½, but it can be handled with some judicious wedging out of battens and cheek pieces on the stem in this area.

Years ago I built a number of semi-stock Hunt-type deep-V 22-footers whose topsides were lapstrake planked, and I hardly need mention that there was no way one could form that conical bow with lapstrake planking. The way I got around that was by planking the first boat to a certain station with the planks hanging out forward a couple of inches. Then I made a plaster plug of the nose from there forward, took a mold off the plug, and provided the boats with a fiberglass "nose cone" that was rabbeted to accept the planking. This, as do so many things, seems a bit trivial, looking back on it after so many years, but it was a good solution to a real problem in the context of its time. This was when lapstrake was "acceptable" and fiberglass was only interesting for what could be done with it. I could fill a page with lessons learned in building that one line of boats, but the only one that applies to lofting is that while you can't build some shapes the way you want, you can build them some way if you want to badly enough. As I mentioned earlier, sometimes it is actually easier to carve out a shape than to draw it and build it, despite all the remarks to the contrary throughout this book. You don't *always* have to be consistent if you don't want to. As any lawyer can tell you, the truth has many faces.

9 / Developing Transoms

Transoms come in so many configurations that it would be unfair to label them all as difficult to loft. In practice, it seems that the more beautiful they are, the more intricate their lofting is. "Intricate" is nearer the truth than "difficult," for taken alone, each step of any transom's lofting is easy to understand. It's just that on some transoms there are so many steps that you may have trouble remembering them all and in what sequence to use them. When this happens, you are likely to make mistakes, work yourself up to a mental block, and give the job a bad name.

Lofting a Plumb Transom

A plumb, flat transom is just a station that happens to be at the end of the lines. It is no more difficult to loft than any other section, nor to pick up than any mould or frame. Given a transom that looks like that shown in Figure 9–1, the body plan view of the transom is the only one you need, for not being raked or curved, this is a true view. Thus your half-pattern is already drawn.

The only information left for you to find is the bevels. In this case, you can find them in the body plan by the three-station method outlined in Chapter 5, measuring normal to the transom between it and the two stations forward of it anywhere along its section. Do this just as was described for floors and frames, except that here you want the bevel of the end station rather than the middle one. Note that you must watch the spacing between the transom and the adjacent station, for it may not be standard, and this different spacing must be reflected in your bevel-finding diagram. To ensure that this is done and also to save time, you can set up for the bevels on these actual station lines in the grid.

Lofting a Raked Transom

A designer only has to rake a flat transom one way or the other to make life a little more interesting for the loftsman. This is so for two reasons. First, not being a straight-line section, the transom is not as easily drawn in the plan view and the body plan as a plumb transom is in these views. And then even when you get the body plan view, you can't use it in making a transom pattern, for it doesn't present a true view of the transom due to the transom's rake. (More on this point later.)

Before drawing the transom in the other views, you should make sure that all the long lines have been drawn and faired. That way when you draw the transom, you can be sure that it won't be involved in any changes that might be necessary to fair the lines. It is for this reason that designers generally omit the offsets of any but the simplest transoms. Instead, they will usually give offsets for a fairing station aft of the transom. The transom can then be "dropped" into the faired lines.

What this means is that to draw the transom, you must get

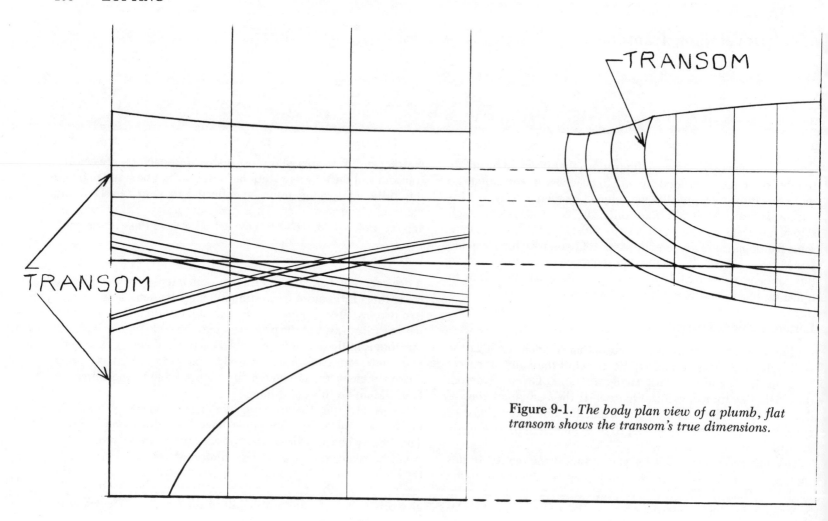

Figure 9-1. *The body plan view of a plumb, flat transom shows the transom's true dimensions.*

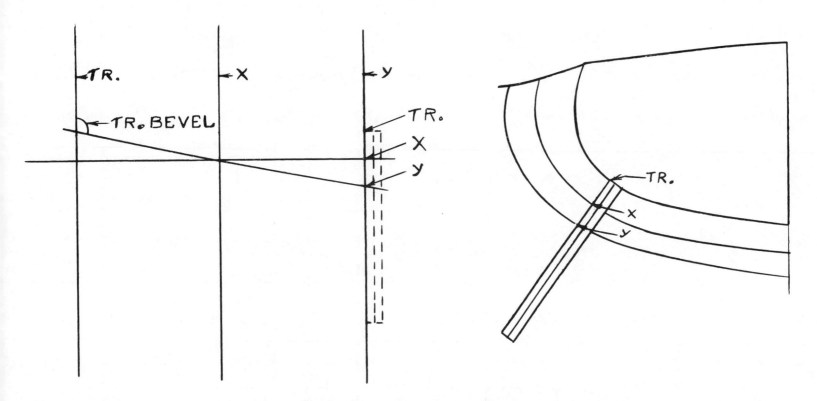

Figure 9-2. *A transom bevel being determined by the three-station method.*

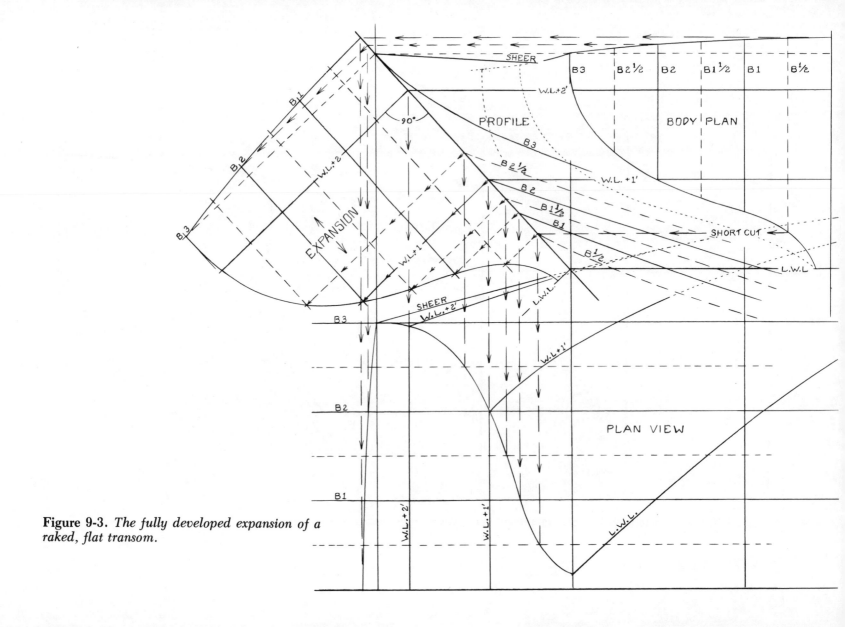

Figure 9-3. *The fully developed expansion of a raked, flat transom.*

heights and half-breadths from information supplied by the faired long lines and their grid-line forms. The procedure was basically described in Chapter 2, but here it is again for good measure:

1. Project the crossings of grid waterlines with the raked transom line in profile into the plan view. There, each such projected intersection results in a point on the outside edge of the transom where the projection intersects with its respective curved waterline. When this projection is extended to the centerline as a line, you have arrived at the transom half-breadth for that waterline. You can then pick up this half-breadth and carry it to the same waterline in the body plan. The offsets for "deck at side" and any other half-breadth on the transom are derived in the same way.

2. Project the buttock long line crossings of the raked transom line in profile down to the plan view, locating them where they intersect the grid buttock lines. These are points on the transom edge. You should also project them as heights from the raked transom line over to the body plan, where their intersections with grid buttocks are the same transom edge points there.

3. When you have enough points to draw in the sections in both of the missing views (there is nothing to stop you from putting in as many extra buttock and waterline long lines as you feel you need to do the shape justice), draw the deck crown atop the body plan view as developed in the deck crown pattern. It must *always* be drawn in the body plan first because only there is the true deck crown shown. You can now take the crown as buttock line heights over to the raked transom line. From there project them into the plan view, where their intersections with the grid buttock lines establish the fore-and-aft location of the transom's crown at the deck level in that view.

To get a true view of the transom for making a pattern, the raked transom must be "expanded," and this is bound to add some confusion. However, it is easy to understand this procedure if you remember that a raked transom is shortened in its vertical dimension in the body plan due to its angle and that when viewed normal to the rake, the transom "expands" to its true vertical dimension. In Figure 9–4, for instance, the height of WL +1′ has "expanded" from 12″ above LWL to 16″ on one transom, and to 20″ on the other.

These are the correct heights for the true or expanded view, and as we saw with the skiff in Chapter 2, if you draw a true view of half of the transom against the transom's profile in the lines so that the two share the same centerline, then automatically all heights on the raked transom's centerline will be correctly located on the true view's centerline. You may wonder why I refer specifically to the flat transom's centerline when the transom's whole after face is represented by one line in the profile. I do this for two reasons: (1) it helps to think of the expanded view as one where half of the transom is rotated at the centerline 90 degrees to the transom profile; and (2) it is a good habit to have when you get to curved transoms, for in those only the centerline is defined in the profile.

If for some reason you don't want to draw the true view against the profile, you can carry the heights of all points as measured along the profile centerline to a separate transom development drawing. Wherever you draw it, you must remember that all heights on it must be "passed through" the raked centerline to find their expanded location in the true view. This is most easily done by relating all heights to waterlines.

Note that rake does not affect half-breadths; they remain the same. The only thing that changes is the relative heights at which they apply because of the difference between measuring heights *up the rake* as opposed to measuring them vertically. Therefore,

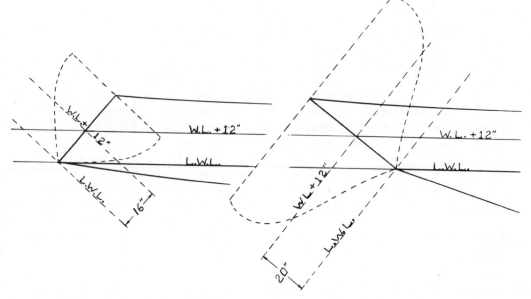

Figure 9-4. *The heights of a raked transom, foreshortened in the profile and body plan views, "expand" to their true dimensions when the transom is projected.*

when you have projected the waterlines out normal to the centerline on the true view, you can tick off their half-breadths right from the half-breadth or the body plans.

It should be apparent, then, that the construction of an expanded half-transom is fairly straightforward. If you feel the need for more points to delineate its edge, you can draw in some additional buttocks or perhaps some extra waterlines, depending upon the transom's shape. In either case, the long lines for fairing these extra lines need not extend more than three stations forward of the transom. In fact, if you are in a hurry and feel that your body plan is fair and true, you can simply draw the additional straight lines in that view and project them directly through the rake of the transom into the true view without drawing their long lines at all. (See dashed "shortcut" line from buttock ½ to transom in Figure 9-3.)

The buttock line spacings, being half-breadths, also remain the same in the true view as in the lines plan. However, the buttock lines' intersections with the transom, both in the hull and in the deck crown, are heights, and these heights must be taken off the raked centerline. That's easy with the hull buttock line endings, which will already be in place, but the deck crown heights must be brought over to the rake from the body plan.

Lofting Curved Transoms

It's interesting to loft a curved transom, and one that is both raked and curved is quite intriguing. But for easier understanding of how to loft the curve, let's consider a plumb, curved transom first.

Here again the lines are usually given to a fairing station, though it may not be out past the stern. Your job is to draw and fair all of the long lines before dropping the transom views into them. When you come to do this, only the centerline of the transom in profile will exist in the lofting; every other point is on a curved surface that you have yet to draw. A transom radius will usually be given somewhere in the plans, and this is often indicated right in the lines profile by a radius line normal to the transom centerline. The radius line being normal to the transom's centerline means that the transom is cylindrical. Of course, it could be elliptical, or any shape, but I can't remember seeing a curved transom that wasn't drawn with a radius, which usually is from one to several times the beam of the stern in length.

Start drawing this transom in the plan view by projecting its centerline from the profile to the plan view's centerline where, being a plumb line, it appears as but a point. Then measure from this point the distance of the transom radius forward along the plan view centerline and from there swing half of the arc of the transom through the transom centerline. That's half of the plumb, curved transom's aft face looking up at it or down at it, as the case may be. (*See* Figure 9–5.)

Naturally, this curve intersects all of the waterlines and the sheer in the plan view at some point, and these are all points on the edge of the transom. It also intersects the grid buttock lines, and these, too, are points on the edge. Therefore, your next move is to project the intersections of the arc and the various long lines right back to the profile, where their intersections with the same named long lines will mark points on the transom's edge in that view. You can then draw in the buttock lines on the transom from their points of intersection with the transom edge up through and above the sheer. They will be parallel to the transom centerline and to one another because they are all longitudinal lines on a cylinder parallel to its axis.

The next step is to draw the body plan view of the transom.

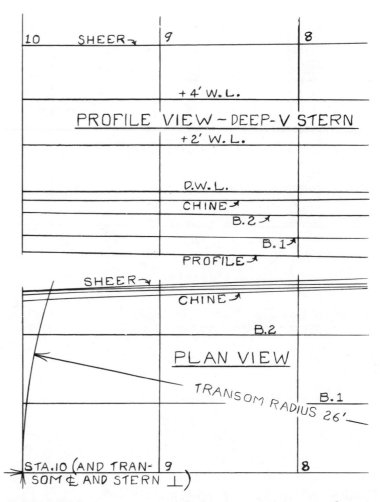

Figure 9-5. *An arc of a given radius swung tangent to the stern perpendicular defines a plumb, curved transom's surface.*

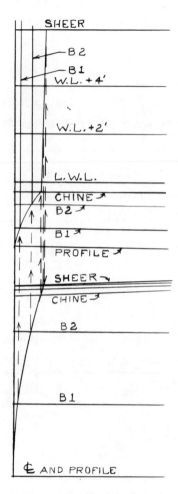

Figure 9-6. *Projecting the transom face/grid line intersections back to the profile to find the outline of the transom in profile.*

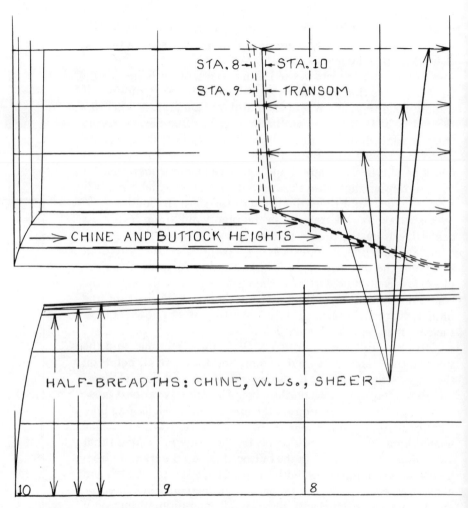

Figure 9-7. *Drawing the body plan view of the transom, taking half-breadths from the plan view and heights from the profile.*

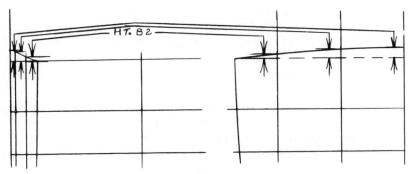

Figure 9-8. *Crown heights taken from body plan to profile.*

First, take the half-breadths of the arc's intersection with the waterlines and sheer into the body plan. Then transfer the heights of the buttock lines at the transom edge from the profile.

At this point, cap the transom in the body plan with the deck crown, using the transom outline's intersection with the deck as a base. Then take its buttock heights over to the profile. On flat-sheered boats, this simply entails projecting the heights over from the body plan, the base height remaining the same all along the curve. Where the transom sits at the end of a rising sheer, however, this simple procedure won't work. Due to the upward sweep of the sheer, the base heights where the crown heights are to be applied will rise as one goes from the outside of the curved

transom toward its middle, i.e., as one gets farther aft. Therefore, when setting off the deck crown heights in such cases, you must use the rising sheerline as your base. The difference between using the straight-line base and the rising one in boats with rising sheers is usually negligible, but if you find any, you must go back to the body plan and correct the transom crown there. (See Figure 9-9 for the difference that can result when the crown heights aren't taken off the true sheer heights.)

Were this a raked transom, your final move to fill out the standard views would be to project these deck crown points from profile to plan view, but in a plumb transom all of these points fall along the same single arc you started out with, so the standard

Figure 9-9. *The difference between projecting over transom crown heights using sheer-based heights and straight line-based heights on a boat with a sweeping sheer. A is the crown measured off the sheerline in the profile. B is the result of projecting crown heights based on a flat line. The error is equal to the incline of the sheer. A^1 is the true body plan view of the transom's top edge. B^1 is the deck crown at the transom/sheerline intersection.*

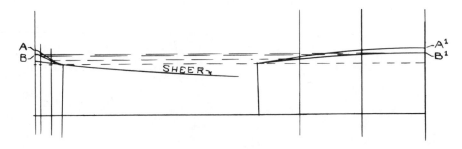

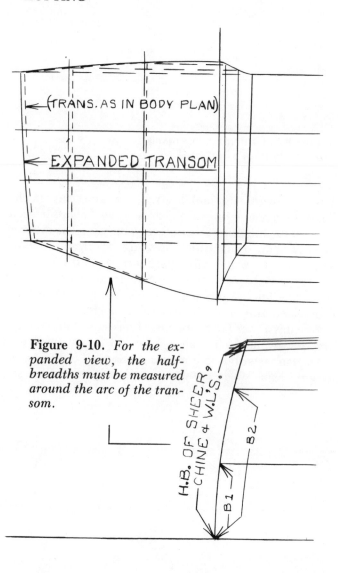

(TRANS. AS IN BODY PLAN)

EXPANDED TRANSOM

H.B. OF SHEER,
CHINE & W.L'S.

B 1

B 2

Figure 9-10. *For the expanded view, the half-breadths must be measured around the arc of the transom.*

views are now completed. You cannot yet start on a transom pattern until you expand, or "roll the curve out flat," so you will want to project an expanded half-transom drawing off its centerline in the profile, much as we did with the raked transom.

Since the transom is plumb, its heights will be unaffected, but all half-breadths will have to be stretched by the amounts that their arcs around the transom are longer than their straight-line half-breadths. What you do, then, after projecting the waterlines out from their intersections with the profile, is to go into the plan view and measure *around the arc* of the transom, from the centerline to its intersection with the desired waterline; this measurement is the half-breadth that you set off in the expanded view. Expand the half-breadths of the sheer and any other horizontal details of the transom by the same method.

As heights are not affected, the buttock line intersections in the expanded view are at the same heights as in the standard views. However, since the buttock line spacings themselves are half-breadths, you must measure around the arc from the centerline in the plan view to each grid buttock line there. These measurements provide the spacing of the buttocks in the expanded view. Unless the curve is sharp, the increase in buttock spacing won't be much, but it does get a bit larger as you go outboard because of the steeper angle at which the arc crosses the parallel lines.

When you have enough points (and you can always put in some more long lines if need be), you will have developed a transom drawing fit for picking up a true pattern—that is, after you make any necessary deductions.

When building the transom you might wish to make a curved form on which to assemble it. If this is the case, you will have some extra lofting to do. This form usually consists of some wide boards or planks longer than the transom's beam. They are cut to its radius less deductions for transom thickness, and perhaps a bit less than that to over-bend the transom so that if the finished product straightens out a little (which it normally does), it will still have the desired curve. These curved pieces are surfaced with rectangular sticks nailed across them. This means that you must furnish either a pattern of the curved base pieces or their radius dimension, remembering to deduct for the thickness of the sticks that are to be nailed atop them.

Lofting a Raked, Curved Transom

As one might expect, the development of a raked, curved transom includes the two types of development that we have discussed separately so far in this chapter: you must expand the heights to accommodate the rake and the half-breadths to "unroll" the curve. That much is fairly straightforward, but because the curve is now tilted out of plumb, a third factor has been introduced, in that it now curves upward or downward, depending on whether the transom is raked aft or forward. The readily seen effects of this are that the curves of the transom's plan view waterlines are no longer the arc of the transom, being stretched fore and aft by the rake; that every point not on the centerline swings up or down as the transom curls up or rolls out flat; and that the waterlines on the expanded transom come out sweeping upward or downward, not as straight lines. (*See* Figure 9–11.) The waterlines, then, distort as the curved transom is tilted.

Fortunately, the transom's buttock lines show only the same spread forward in the profile and the same spread apart on the expanded transom that we saw on the plumb transom. They remain straight, parallel, and in the same fore-and-aft relationship to the centerline, regardless of rake. Therefore, they are useful as a constant or "handle" in constructing the curved plane of the transom and in locating its intersections in the standard views.

Starting with a set of hull lines that have been faired except for the transom—there is nothing but the profile centerline and a

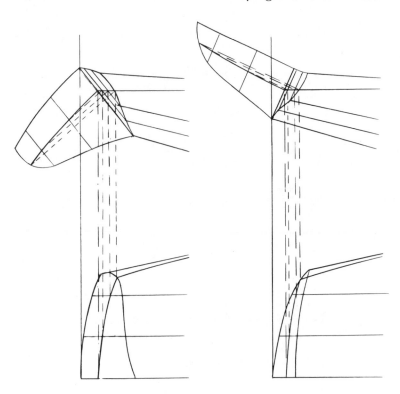

Figure 9-11. *Waterlines on raked, curved transoms are curved.*

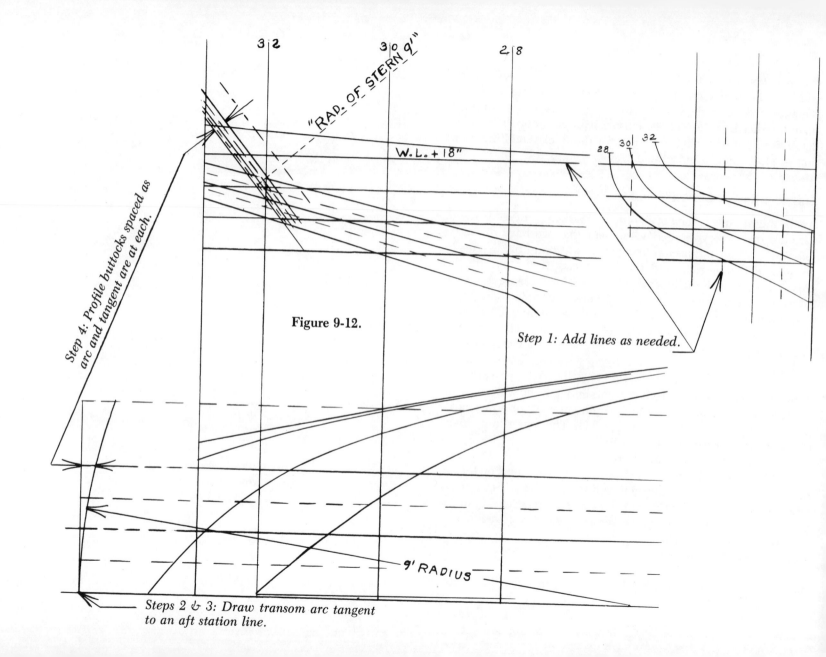

32   30   "RAD. OF STERN 9"   28

28   30   32

W.L. + 18"

Step 4: Profile buttocks spaced as arc and tangent are at each.

Figure 9-12.

Step 1: Add lines as needed.

9' RADIUS

Steps 2 & 3: Draw transom arc tangent to an aft station line.

given radius for this—you can drop in the standard views as outlined in the following series of steps (Figures 9-12–9-18):

1. Make sure that there are sufficient buttocks and waterlines cutting through the transom to define its shape. Draw in any extras that you feel are necessary to fill extensive gaps in the transom perimeter and fair them through two stations forward of the aftermost station.
2. Set up a station in the plan view well abaft the transom, and extend the grid buttocks to it.
3. Draw the arc of the transom tangent to this station by setting off its radius from the station forward along the centerline.
4. Pick up the distance on each buttock line between the tangent station and the transom arc, set these off forward of the transom centerline in the profile, and draw the transom's buttock lines through the resulting points parallel to the centerline. The intersections of these profile transom buttocks with their respective long lines are points on the edge of the transom, and these points will project into both plan view and body plan to find transom edge points at their intersections with the grid buttocks of those views.
5. From the profile, project into the plan view the crossings of a waterline with the transom's centerline and with each transom buttock line. Draw the waterline through these points out to its intersection with its same-named long line. This intersection yields a point on the edge of the transom in that view and by projection a point on the transom edge in the profile view. It helps to realize that as parallel planes cutting a cylinder, all plan view waterlines that cross the transom will be the same shape and parallel to one another. Therefore, once one is drawn, you have only to project a single point of the others from the profile to fix their fore-and-aft locations and then draw them parallel to the first

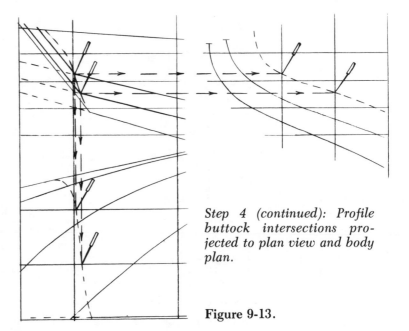

Step 4 (continued): Profile buttock intersections projected to plan view and body plan.

Figure 9-13.

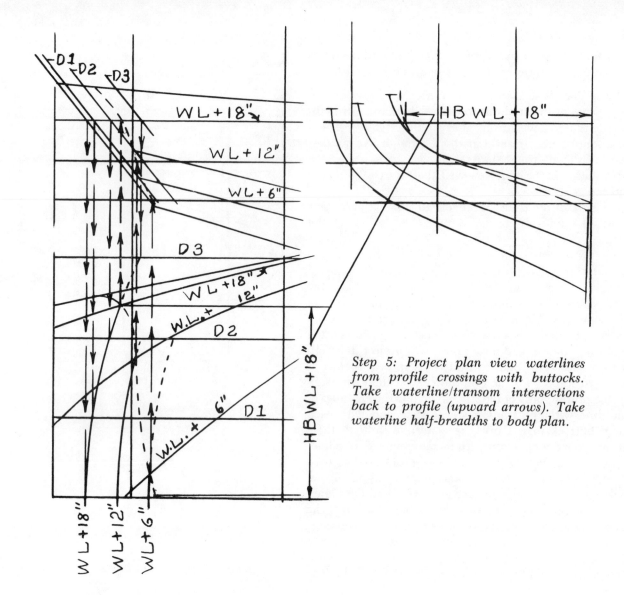

Figure 9-14.

Step 5: Project plan view waterlines from profile crossings with buttocks. Take waterline/transom intersections back to profile (upward arrows). Take waterline half-breadths to body plan.

line. For that reason, you might draw the widest transom waterline first. To ensure the greatest accuracy in drawing this first waterline, it is sometimes wise to put an extra buttock line out past the widest waterlines.

6. Should the sheer at the transom be parallel to the waterline—and there have always been some such boats, although fortunately not many during my impressionable years—you would locate the intersection of sheer and transom the same as with any other waterline's intersection with its respective long line. But when it is sweeping up, or even down, you will have to project its profile transom crossings into the plan view and construct its own peculiar curve across the transom there until it intersects its long line. For results that are exactly right, you should do this with the faired extension of the sheer through or past the transom in both views. It is important to realize that you are not drawing the actual transom top, but just a line to fix the transom's intersection with the sheer.

7. With the buttock, waterline, and sheer intersections all found in either the profile or plan views and those missing in one view filled in by projection from the other, you have enough points to draw the transom edges (except for the transom top) in both views. Once drawn in these views, you can then draw the transom section in the body plan, taking its half-breadths from the plan view and its heights from the profile.

8. After the body plan view is drawn up to the sheer, you can put in the deck crown and then take it over to the profile view. There are two things to remember about this. First, do not draw this crown until the correct sheer height and half-breadth have been found by constructing the other two standard views as we have done in the preceding steps, for otherwise the "base" you use for drawing the intersection of

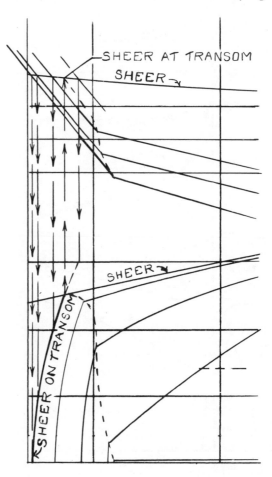

Figure 9-15.

Step 6: Draw sheer in plan view and project transom/sheer intersection back to profile.

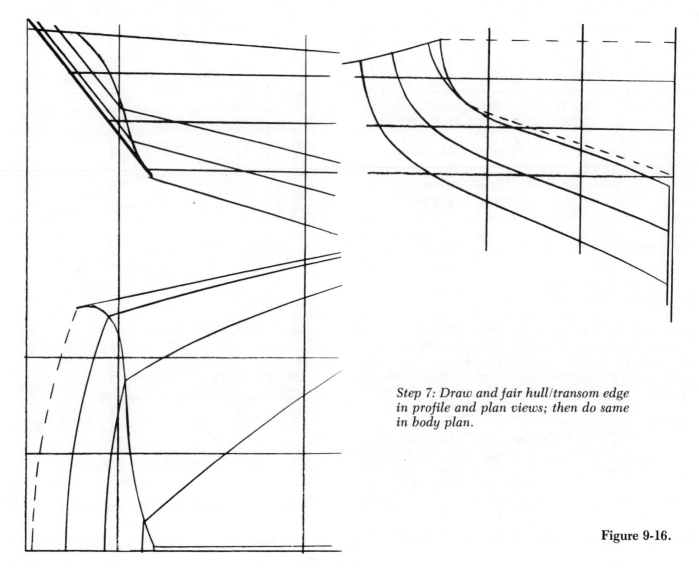

Step 7: Draw and fair hull/transom edge
in profile and plan views; then do same
in body plan.

Figure 9-16.

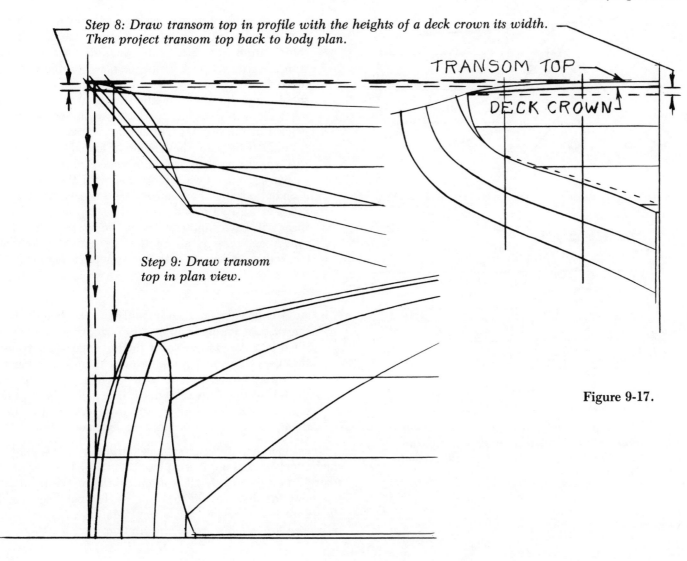

Step 8: Draw transom top in profile with the heights of a deck crown its width. Then project transom top back to body plan.

TRANSOM TOP

DECK CROWN

Step 9: Draw transom top in plan view.

Figure 9-17.

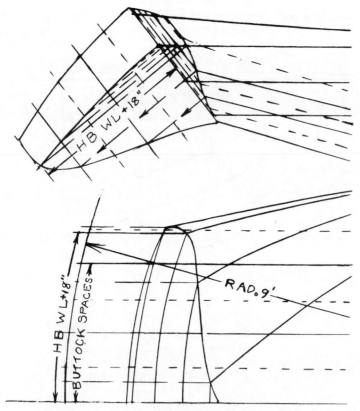

Step 10: Draw expanded half-transom. Space buttocks and measure half-breadths around arc of transom radius. Project all heights from profile normal to transom centerline.

Figure 9-18.

your crown may not be accurate. It might be different if you were given the sheer intersection and told, "The transom is from here aft." But when all you are given is a transom with its back against a raked profile and its arms hooked out to catch a sheer that is angling in on it, you should use the above method so that you know exactly where to start drawing the deck crown. Second, when the heights of the deck crown are taken into the profile view from the body plan, they should be added to (measured vertically up from) the sheer, as extended through the transom, to mark the crown's intersection with the centerline and each buttock line. Remember, this is necessary when there is much aft rake, a round stern, or a steep sheer, because the sheer will have climbed some in the distance that the transom's centerline is aft of the transom at side, and the transom should climb with it so as not to look too low. Don't forget to check and correct the curve in the body plan if necessary.

9. After connecting our set of profile crown heights with the line of the transom's top or deck edge, you can now project them into the plan view for the top edge of the transom in that view. This brings you full circle in the construction of the three standard views, and when you are satisfied that the line of the transom's edge is true and fair—even though sometimes it may look a little strange in shape—in all of them, you are ready to draw an expanded view.

Once again with this curved, raked transom, you should look to the buttock lines as a starting place. Assuming that you are going to project an expanded half-transom off the centerline in the profile view, the first move is to set up the buttock lines parallel to the centerline, spacing them out from it their distances as measured *around the arc* of the transom. Right away you will reap a set of points on the transom edge by simply projecting each transom profile buttock's intersection with the transom edge over to the same-named buttock in the expanded view. Since these points are all projected normal to the centerline and buttocks of the profile, you can carry over the heights using either a large square or by setting them off a squared reference line.

With the buttock points done, only the waterlines and the sheer remain. As mentioned before, these cross the face of the expanded transom as curves, and you plot the path of each by projecting its crossings with each buttock in the profile view over to the same-named expanded buttock. But when you come to project its end or transom edge point, you must get an expanded half-breadth for it. This requires that you project its half-breadth in the plan view aft to our transom arc drawing and then measure around the arc for the expanded half-breadth. All waterlines in the expanded view will be parallel curves, but the sheer will be a different curve unless it, like the waterlines, is straight and level.

It is a good idea to pick up all of these lines as well as the centerline on the transom pattern and transfer them to the transom itself as locators for the bevels and as aids in setting up the transom in the boat. There is little use in accurately lofting a transom if it is not as accurately set up—raked, leveled, and horned—and some good lines on it are invaluable to that part of the job.

Determining Bevels

Bevels are devils on a shapely transom, and they get worse the more raked the transom is, being compounded if it is also curved. As has been pointed out before, you can take bevels along the long lines if you are careful to hold the bevel square in the plane of the long line and its grid line on the transom. However, I have never been happy with this method. It always seems to introduce just enough error so that the transom needs a little fixing up when I get it into place, especially if it is sharply raked and curved and of fairly thick stock.

In an effort to make the bevels come out just right I have used a procedure that amounts to lofting the transom three times: once for its aft face, once for the forward face of the transom planking, and once for the forward face of the cheek pieces. This not only works better, it produces bevels that are, in fact, just about exactly right. If one can take the time—and it really doesn't take that much longer—going around three times and making three half-patterns is certainly the best way to go. It may be fun for some boatbuilders to stand under the boat and work down something left oversize, but it's a joy to the loftsman when the transom is put up in place and nothing has to be done to it.

The situation on shapely transoms with rake and curve is not made any easier by the hull planking deductions. You cannot make the deductions straight in from the edge of the expanded view; this would understate the deduction in proportion to the amount that the transom was expanded. Instead you must make the deductions in the body plan view as you have done with all the stations. Then, to get the true ready-to-construct shape, pick up the offsets of the deducted section along waterlines and buttocks. This way, you should come out with about the same amount of DAE as the aft stations have—that's what makes a fair hull.

Since that process is rather lengthy, I have tried the following method: At those places along the developed transom's outline where the amount of the deduction is wanted, set a bevel square at the angle that would extend the transom's bevel aft (180 degrees minus the angle of the transom bevel). Then lay a planking-thickness fid against the bevel square, its outer face in line with the transom outline, and mark the necessary deduction at the inner face of the fid. This works as well as any method.

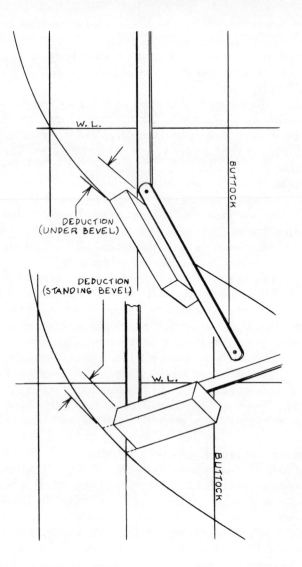

When using accurate bevels, this method results in deductions that are just right. Further, the bevels have to be pretty far out before the resultant error in deduction is noticeable, and if they're that far out you've blown the lofting anyway.

While obviously not all there is to it, the above procedures are about all you have to do to get the job of developing a transom done. I regret if I have contributed toward any confusion of terms that may have different usages in different localities; I have tried to keep the language as plain and homogeneous as possible to avoid misinterpretation from shifting terms. Anyway, I have enjoyed this chapter perhaps more than any other as a challenge to put into words—not just into drawings—many things that I have done and taught for many years, yet about which there has always been that skulking doubt whether I really understood all that I knew about it well enough to explain it without actually doing and showing it on the floor.

It is possible that you will run into some transoms that are quite different from those covered here. There have been boats with two transom faces (one under and at an angle to the other), boats with round sterns like a tugboat's, boats with pointy transoms, boats with Oriental open sterns with a recessed transom, and modern things with no transom to speak of from the cockpit sole up. Whatever type of stern it is, if you bear in mind the basic principle of dropping the transom into the faired hull lines, of building it out from where it sits until it meets the long lines, you will be able to do it. After all, as I have been known to say around the shop, no matter what the problem, "It's only a boat."

Figure 9-19. *Establishing the bevels with planking fid and bevel square.*

One-offs

To the loftsman, a one-off fiberglass boat can mean easy living, since much of the detail work required to fully loft a wooden or steel boat will not be needed. What is wanted is the shape of the boat—the true shape, to be sure—but only the shape as embodied in the simplest form or mold on or in which the boat will be built. For this you will need only a minimum of bevels, few, if any, rabbets, and patterns for just one edge of the pieces.

Mold or Form?

The many systems for building a one-off fiberglass hull or deck fall into two basic types: those built *inside* a throw-away mold (a female mold) and those built on the *outside* of a throw-away form (a male mold). The main difference between the two is that at the end of the laminating, a "part" taken from a mold exactly reflects the mold's shape and surface, while a "part" made on a form, having been built up layer by layer on the outside, has become slightly less like the form with each successive layer and needs fairing and smoothing and the application of exterior paint or gelcoat.* Since getting a good finish on raw fiberglass is slow,

---

*A "part" in fiberglass jargon is any single molded piece, be it a hull, deck, or just a hatch.

fussy work compared to spraying or brushing gelcoat into a mold with relative abandon, it is a well-known axiom in the trade that, where applicable, "any mold is better than a form."

The choice of mold or form, then, boils down to the cost of surfacing the mold's interior versus the cost of putting a finish on the raw fiberglass hull. Compared to a part built on a form, the cost of a one-off molded part is always cheaper when dealing with flat surfaces or "developable" curves. For example, who would build a skiff like the 12-footer described in Chapter 2 on a form, spending the time to put a good finish on it, when he could make it in an almost identical mold (except for being built inside out) and take out a part as smooth and fair as the material facing the mold's interior? Who cares to compete, using sandpaper and paint, with the high polish of a sheet of Formica? This reasoning holds for all parts having mostly flat, radiused, or developable surfaces.

However, as the amount of compound, difficult-to-surface-or-plank curvature increases in a part, at some point it becomes more expensive to use a mold than a form. The cost turning-point with powerboat hulls comes after the usual flat- and V-bottomed types and is about at the Hunt-designed deep-V shape of Chapter 6. A mold could easily be built for the after half of such a boat, but the extreme compound curvature of the bow would be so difficult to plank and would require so much surfacing of the mold or the part that the advantage of the mold over a form might be easily wiped out. In sailboats the cost turning point comes in any models more complex than boats like the Star, the 210, or the Meadow Lark, as I can attest, having made one-off molds for several boats of this radiused-bottomed type. These things can change with the development of new methods, however, and what I say here could be wrong tomorrow.

Perhaps that's enough boatbuilding talk for a book on lofting. However, I have always felt that too many one-off parts are made the hard way. There is little question that this is due not only to a lack of understanding of the material, or of how much easier it is to mold than to finish, but also to a lack of familiarity with lofting, of being able to recognize that molds are just as easy to loft and set up as anything else from a given lines plan. After all, it's exactly the same thing; it's just on the other side of the line.

One-off Deck Molds

Because of its many easily developed surfaces and the quantity of detail, a deck with trunk and cockpit lends itself more than any other one-off part to being built on a mold rather than on a form. The quantity of detail also means that an extensive job of lofting can hack away many, many hours of labor from the building job. The opportunities in such a mold for fabricating details that will become prefinished parts of a finished structure are almost endless, even as they are on a production deck. A hole in the mold, framed beneath, becomes a hatch coaming or mast collar, and depressions can form coamings or winch pads. A stick of wood and two wedges tacked on become neat cockpit seat drains . . . (there I go boatbuilding again). Anyway, it's the loftsman who makes it all possible.

To build a one-off deck mold, proceed as follows. (I will assume that the major part of the lofting has been completed.) Start at the sheer of the lines plan on the floor and if there is a given, uniform crown, draw the deck crown at every station in the body plan. Then draw the deck's centerline (the top of the deck's crown) in the profile and check its fairness. On some boats an unpleasant hump or hollow may appear in the foredeck, or more rarely, in the after deck. This is a product of the sweep of the sheer, the changing width of the deck, and the lessening crown as the deck narrows. When you find such an unfairness, there is nothing to do but doctor the crown on certain stations to conform with a fair deck centerline profile, and if necessary you can fair the problem area further with a short buttock line or two.

Because of this unfairness (which certain hull types are prone to) as well as for reasons pertaining to headroom, visibility, rating rule advantages or constraints, a designer will sometimes give you a "top of deck at centerline" measurement in the plans in lieu of a uniform crown. This calls for differing amounts of crown all along the boat so the deck will fit between the given deck at side and deck at centerline measurements. An easy way to draw these crowns is to use a drawing aid made up of two boards, each a little longer than the boat's greatest beam, nailed together like the rafters of a pitched roof at an angle to fit the three points through which you are to draw the crown. If you put a pencil in the apex and slide the boards from side to side against the two picks in the deck at side points, you get a crown with the proper height and width. Of course, if the boat is so wide as to make this a clumsy business, you can do it at a fractional size and scale it up to full size. You can also draw each crown by any of the usual methods on the stations in the body plan, and you can even draw some deck buttock lines if a great number of intermediate points are going to be needed. This, however, is more likely to happen on a boat with many deck beams than on a one-off mold.

With the main deck drawn in the body plan and profile, and already extant in the plan view, you can now proceed to outline

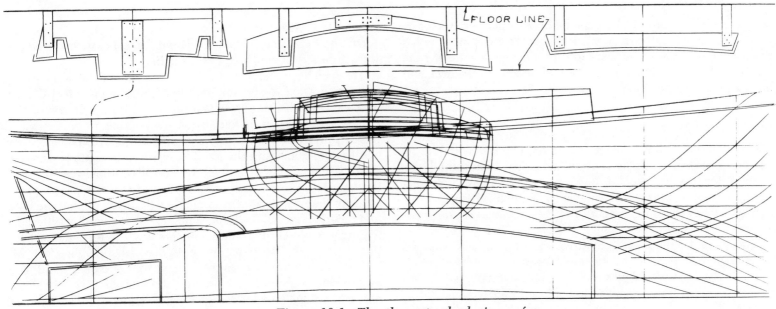

Figure 10-1. *The three standard views of a cabin trunk and cockpit and some plywood moulds for a one-off deck mold.*

the trunk, coamings, cockpit well, seat lockers, hatches, and other features as these appear in the three views. Obviously, the ends of each structure, and any other athwartship faces or jogs that don't happen to fall on a station, will require their own section or partial section drawings.

Once all of the structures you wish to include in the one-off deck are outlined and faired, you can add on for the skin of the mold plus stringers where these are employed, put in a floor line over the body plan, and build the moulds for the mold. When these are set up, stringered and cleated as necessary, and skinned over, the loftsman's next job is to lay out for the carpenters such details as the scuppers, hatch coamings and drains, mast holes,

portlight holes, and winch and other hardware bases. He must also locate all of the other hardware and trim, like handrails, cleats, blocks, travelers and jib tracks, and chainplates, so that a non-skid pattern can be shaped to leave smooth areas around them.

When the mold is turned over to some good fiberglass men, you should end up with the finest kind of one-piece deck. It may not be as slick as some production job whose plug and mold were polished to the nth degree, but it will be just as functional, and better in many ways than anything built one-off on the boat. And, by the time all details are individually fabricated on the latter, it is cheaper, too. Another advantage of the molded one-off deck is that a one-off, form-built hull can be built in place on top of it, and if you have a bulwark on the deck, or take the trouble with a deck that is to have no bulwark to turn a flange down along the topsides, then you can laminate the hull directly to the deck and have a one-piece boat.

One-Off Hull Forms

In lofting a hull that is to be built on a form, it is essential, as in all lofting, that the loftsman know what construction method is to be used, for it will make a difference in what he has to pick up and in how he will make his deductions. Without getting into the various one-off building methods in detail, I can point out that some materials like C-Flex planking can be applied directly to the bulkheads and moulds without stringers, while others, such as those that use an Airex core, might call for stringers. If the former were the case, you would pick up all the bulkheads plus whatever moulds were necessary to fill in in between. This would call for deducting the width of the skin from the bulkheads and moulds. If the latter were the case, you would have to deduct for both the skin and the stringers on the moulds, while for the bulkheads, you would have to deduct only for the skin, since the stringers would be notched into them. Bulkheads are often padded to prevent them from "printing" through a single-skin hull as the tabbing shrinks and pulls them too tightly against the hull. If so, the pads must be deducted as well. Some builders will leave the bulkheads out of the setup rather than notch the stringers through them, for removing the stringers can be a nasty job unless one had the forethought to shim them in place in an oversize notch. There is even a system where the stringers are left in and covered with glass, the spaces between the stringers being filled in with insulating foam and the whole layer covered with an inner skin. Almost everything you can think of has been tried, but whatever the

system, the loftsman must understand how it will be assembled, used, and torn apart, or somebody will have a more involved job than necessary somewhere along the line.

The backbone members found in wooden and metal boats all but vanish when you get into building forms for one-offs. All that is needed is something to which the ends of the stringers or the C-Flex planking can be fastened. Usually, a board on edge or a piece of plywood cut out to the profile of the fore keel and stem and let into notches in the moulds, or fitted in sections between them, will do. For a deep keel, the side pieces should overlap the flat board that forms the bottom. Otherwise, if the bottom piece overlaps the side pieces, the laminate will shrink around the bottom board and it will be impossible to remove it without literally tearing it to pieces. This is a common mistake in forming the bottom of any box-like structure around which fiberglass will be laminated. For instance, in the cockpit well of a deck mold, the side pieces should cover the ends of the bottom piece, or there may be a struggle with it despite the most generous "draft" (taper of the part for removal from the mold) and radiusing of the corners. Also, the middle of the panels of such a box or any large flat surface, such as a flat transom, should be well bolstered if not deliberately shored out to a slight convexity. Otherwise the laminate, hanging up on the corners as it shrinks, will force the panel inward, producing a "dished-in" surface, which is particularly unattractive. Again I am getting into boatbuilding matters (next time I'll do a book on boatbuilding).

When you come to the transom of the one-off form, you can go any of several routes to get the shape. What you don't need is anything as complete or substantial as what is needed for a wood transom; you just need an accurately shaped structure or form. For a boat with a flat transom, the simplest way to go is probably to cut the form out of plywood. The plywood can be relatively thin and only "good one side"; don't forget to throw a slight

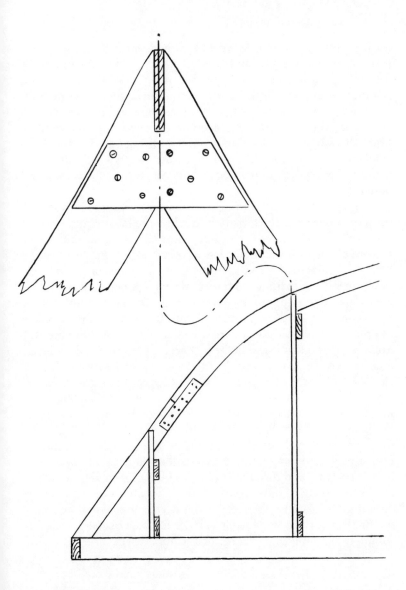

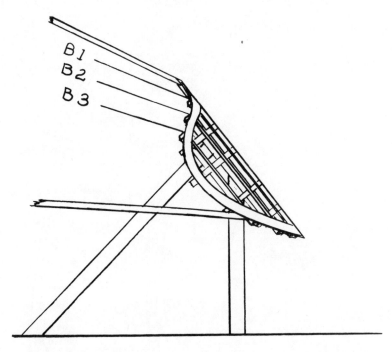

Above: Figure 10-3. *A one-off transom form.*

Left: Figure 10-2. *The backbone structure for a one-off form.*

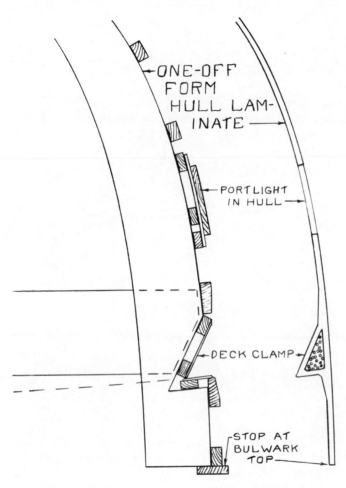

Figure 10-4. *A form with integral hull features built into it.*

athwartship crown in it to avoid a dished-in laminate. A curved transom might well be laminated of plywood, but it can also be formed by, in effect, setting up the rack on which you would laminate it in place in the form. Such a rack would best be built of athwartship pieces sawn to the transom's radius, less deductions with vertical stringers placed on the centerline and buttock lines; this carries check points from the lofting onto the form. To catch the ends of the stringers, a border of plywood cut to the transom pattern's shape can be put on the aft face of the rack and notched.

Putting all this boatbuilding aside and returning to lofting, the primary concern of the loftsman should be to lay out and provide for every detail that can be built into the form so that every feature of the hull is more or less automatically completed as the boat is laminated. He can save the builders many hours of trimming, grinding, drilling, and secondary glass bonding if he does not allow the setup to be rushed together and a hull to be prematurely splashed over it. Granted, the opportunities are not as great as in a mold for incorporating details, but there are still areas where you can save labor by careful planning, and they all add up. For instance, there is little excuse for having to trim a raw sheerline when a stop can be installed on the form at a fraction of the cost. Other such examples include the following: having to build on a sheer or bulwark top flange that could have been laminated in place; having to grind away and build up glass to form a fairwater ahead of the propeller or a recess for the rudder heel fitting; and having to cut and drill out a propeller aperture, hull portlights, and through-hull holes in the finished hull. When the loftsman could have established the locations of, and gotten out plugs or forming pieces for, these details to make things right the first time, the only possible excuses for such oversights are incomplete planning, ignorance, or incompetence.

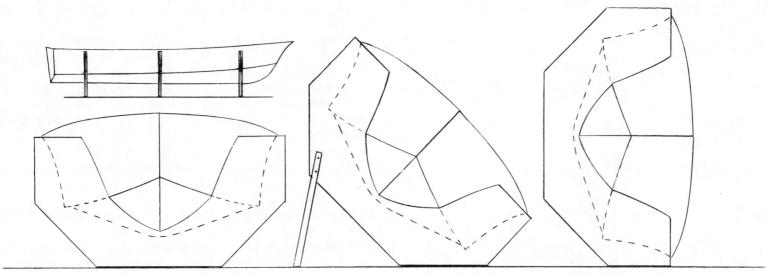

Figure 10-5. *Rocker bulkheads for turning molds.*

One-Off Hull Molds

When you build a one-off hull mold, not only can you incorporate most details of the exterior quite easily, but you also have the advantage of producing them with a gelcoat finish, which means that the detail is truly finished and done with. Even with this method, however, you will have extra work if you don't plan well. I once helped sort out the production tooling for some small powerboats and found that these boats had been coming out of the molds for years with a flange that had to be trimmed off each hull and deck before the two could be put together in a no-flange "coffee can" joint. Just as with a form-built hull, installing stops would have meant a significant saving, as well as a product without raw, uneven edges to be mated and somehow buried.

As mentioned and sketched in our discussion of deductions in Chapter 3, the best way to get an understanding of the mold's add-ons before picking up its moulds is to make a full-size detail sketch from the outside of the hull outward. If you do this on the midship section in the body plan, you will see not only where the lining material and stringers will position the inboard edge of the moulds, you will also see what sort of stock will be appropriate, judging by this largest mould. You should also draw a floor line under the body plan and lay out the "rockers," the two moulds—or three for big boats—that will be built larger than the others and have several flat spots on which the mold can rest in various positions for easy access during lamination. Place the two or three rockers on stations that divide the boat roughly into three or four parts and make them bigger than the mould of the midship sec-

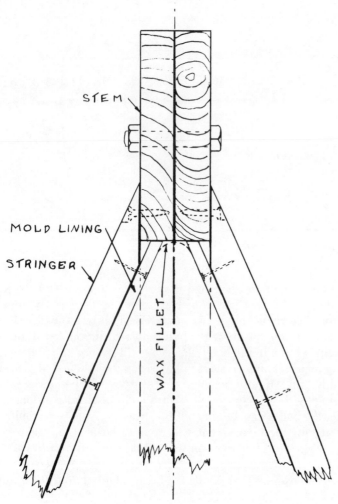

STEM

MOLD LINING

STRINGER

WAX FILLET

Figure 10-6. *The stem assembly of a split mold.*

tion (lest it bump the floor). They should have identical shapes so that the mold is not distorted when resting in the various positions. Needless to say, a similar arrangement can be handy on a deck mold, too, as size and configuration can make parts of it inaccessible. However, the shape of a deck mold is not as inherently stiff as a hull mold, and it may need bracing if it is to be set in any but the "as built" position.

The transom of a mold is drawn and developed just as it might be for a one-off form, except that it is picked up and built from the outside looking in. The same is done with the stem. This part of the mold can be visualized most easily as a piece extending forward of the face of the hull's stem against which the mold lining material fits and onto which the stringers fasten. Note that Figure 10–6 shows the mold's stem to be of two pieces bolted together. Molds are best built in halves due to the increased accessibility to the mold's inside that this method offers. It also means that such tight areas as the keel and stem can be worked on more easily.

Production Tooling

The loftsman's part in fiberglass tooling is similar to his work in one-off construction; the end product is usually a plug, a perfectly shaped and polished pattern of the hull and/or deck, on which a mold or molds for the part can be built. Usually, the plug will never be launched, which means that it can be built the easiest possible way and with whatever materials that best define the shape. Sometimes, however, a prototype boat will be built and tried out, and when all is satisfactory, a mold will be taken from it. When you remember how many flawed models have been rushed into production and sold by the dozens, or even hundreds, before any were used enough to discover their faults, you can't knock that approach.

The ideal way to build a prototype is one-off in fiberglass

because of its similarity to the final product, its relative ease of alteration, and the stability of that material as a base for the clean detail and fair surfaces that are the hallmark of good fiberglass boatbuilding. Due to the stability and the excellent durability of the material, plugs are also sometimes built one-off in fiberglass, and most wooden plugs are at least thinly covered with fiberglass. Anyway, most production molds are made from plugs rather than from prototypes, and most plugs are basically wooden, with a trend toward fiberglass plugs and fiberglass-covered wooden plugs. To the loftsman, this all sifts down to about the same degree of complexity, or lack of it, in his work, and regardless of how the plug is built, the industry's attitude toward tooling is always the same—they want the molds as soon as possible.

You should not infer from the relatively simple building techniques that accuracy is not important. As pointed out elsewhere, when hundreds or thousands of boats will bear the stamp of the plug, it can certainly use all the perfection of line that can be translated into it from the design. And you can be pretty sure if you are lofting the "All New SuperCruiser 33" for Conglomerated International that the designer will come by to have a look.

The complete lofting of hull plugs requires that you give consideration to certain construction considerations: the plug should have enough moulds to support its planking material without showing its "bones"; it should have good markings to facilitate a true setup; and it should have a stiff base to minimize distortion when the plug is moved or transported. Nor should plugs be built too lightly, because not only is a substantial weight of fiberglass used in making a mold on them, but the shrinkage of the material, especially if it is built up too quickly, can apply considerable force anywhere it can get a grip to squeeze the structure. On some boats this can result in an excessively hollow entrance; in others with tumblehome aft, the result can be an hourglass effect just forward of the transom; and on a chine boat

with little or no keel, the laminate, stretched from chine to chine like a bow string, can actually hog its bottom along the centerline. I was on hand when the hull mold of a 22-foot outboard developed a hog as lamination progressed. After the mold was removed, the plug was not hogged, and this puzzled me until I finally realized that the plug had simply sprung back to its original shape once the pressure had been removed.

The matters of draft (the taper that allows removal of parts from molds) and the tendency of flat panels to dish inward are, of course, much more critical in tooling than in one-offs; so the loftsman should keep an eye out for such potential problems. Naturally, there are innumerable other areas of concern peculiar to fiberglass production boats, such as what thickness deck laminate should be allowed for when the deck is to fit over the hull, what radii to use on edges and on "in-corners," and how to treat openings, to name but three of the most common problems. The way these and other details are handled vary widely with different fiberglass plants, and all I can say is that, while it helps to have experience with various fiberglass production methods, it is never safe to take even the smallest detail for granted or to assume that it will be handled as you have done it or seen it done before. It is far better to head off possible recriminations later by finding out exactly what it is that the builders are assuming you will do about these things.

Production molds are often built so that they split down the centerline. To prepare a plug for this, you must loft and pick up a "fence" that will fit the plug on one side of the centerline. The fence is temporarily fastened to the plug until one side of the mold has been laminated up against it. It is then removed and the other half of the mold is laid up against the flange formed by the fence on the first piece. Though bolts may be used to hold the split mold together, the bolt holes will eventually wear out and allow the pieces to slip a little. To avoid a mismatch of the two halves of

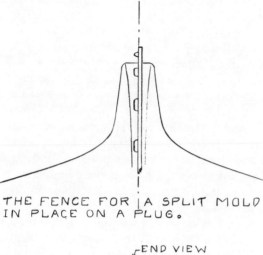

THE FENCE FOR A SPLIT MOLD
IN PLACE ON A PLUG.

END VIEW

TWO PROPERLY SHAPED KEYS.

Figure 10-7.

Figure 10-8. *A split rudder plug mounted on a fence.*

production molds, "keys" can be installed on the fence. These may be truncated prisms or hemispherical bumps (as long as they are easy to clean out), duplicated on the opposite half as matching bumps and cavities, that will accurately position the mold pieces relative to one another. For rudders, centerboards, trunks, skegs, or any other thin parts likely to be built in a split mold, it may be easier to make a split plug and then fit the halves to a smooth sheet, rather than to try to make a fence around the edge.

Perhaps I am again drifting into more boatbuilding than lofting, but, as I have tried to stress, the line is not easily drawn. It is also true that the loftsman, or the loftsman in us boatbuilders, is rarely used enough. All too often a set of moulds and patterns is whisked out of the loft as soon as there is enough to go on, resulting in too many details bluffed into existence on the job when a little more quiet study in the loft would have turned them out quickly and easily and exactly right. So what if the vice president of Conglomerated wants to know the status of the plug. Don't rush things to "make a showing"; he can afford ulcers better than you can. Always have a few questions about details ready. It's like throwing a handful of grass on the doorstep of a beehive: it keeps those who would rush you so busy that they forget what they were angry about.

Sooner or later in his career a loftsman will take the lines off an existing boat, either for use in building another one or possibly just for posterity's sake. Certainly nobody is more qualified to do this than a loftsman—not even a designer, who could always be suspected of "improving" her here or there. It's an enjoyable job, rarely undertaken with other than an interesting boat. It hardly ever happens at a convenient time or place or with the boat in a convenient position, but the latter is easily overcome with a little improvisation.

What you need to remember about taking the lines off a boat is what I said in Chapter 2: with the stem, the stern, a number of station sections, and a handle on all the "bumps" in the profile, you've got it all. With this in mind, one of your first moves upon arriving on the scene should be to mark off the boat into whatever number of stations you feel will accurately define her shape. A regular spacing is not necessary; it is more important that you avoid obstructions like cradle arms or boats too close on both sides that make measurement difficult and that you deliberately land stations to cover certain important features, such as breaks in the deck or the ends of trunks. With a little study, you will see that each boat obviously has some good and bad station locations for measuring in situ.

The very first move is to determine how nearly level the boat is. It would be handy, but just short of amazing, if she were level both athwartships and fore and aft. Despite the ease with which boats can be shifted today, it might not be worthwhile to level her up fore and aft, but except for the heaviest vessels, she can probably be straightened up athwartships fairly easily. This can be checked with a straightedge and level across the deck in a couple of places, with a plumb bob off the ends lined up with the hull's centerline, or even with a level against the bulkheads and joinerwork down below.

Should you have to leave her all awry, so be it, but that doesn't mean you'll go home empty-handed; measurements can still be taken by a variety of methods when the boat is out of level. True, it does make it more difficult to obtain sheer heights when a transit, sight level, or water level is used. However, it will not hamper taking them off with a taut reference line or wire above the deck, nor will it affect the method that I advocate of picking up the station sections. Taking the sections off at an angle shouldn't disturb you if you recall that many old-time "draughtsmen" drew and set up their vessels with the waterlines running downhill relative to the stations. Remember that after you draw and fair the lines using whatever stations you take off, you can put in any other stations and long lines you want. This means that if the sections were taken off at an angle, you could still drop into the faired lines some perpendicular stations from which to make moulds.

Once you have decided where to locate the stations, you should mark them along the deck at side and horn them to the other side to get their full breadths, and thereby their half-breadths. What with deck crown and other obstructions, you will usually have to do this between two levels, and if working alone, you may need to block up a straightedge in place and measure up to it. Of course, you might come up with some other trick to do this—even lifeline stanchions have been pressed into service. It doesn't matter if the boat is listing as long as you measure at the same height above the sheer between parallel uprights or levels.

There are many ways to find the heights of the sheer on each station, and as long as the heights are referred to a straight line, which may be above, below, or right through the boat, it doesn't matter whether the boat is level fore and aft. The handiest piece of two-man equipment for taking heights is a transit or a sight level, but for one man the water level is best, and is fairly simple to rig up. With these, the level at which they are set up is the reference line, and you'll have to average the two sides if there is a list. If you lack these tools, it may be possible to rig a taut line above the deck from bow to stern near the centerline. This way, using a straightedge rigged across a station, you can combine the taking of heights with getting the half-breadths.

Still another way to get the sheer heights is to use the waterline as a reference, picking it up as you take off each station, provided that the waterline is straight. You can also stretch a taut line under the boat parallel to the centerline, recording its distance from the centerline and the distance from it to the deck at bow and stern. Just as the waterline does, such a line locates the heights of all points on the sections if it is picked up as you take off each station.

If the many alternatives above seem confusing, they might sort themselves out if I make a simple list of what your objectives should be. But the list, too, will be more meaningful if I first describe how to take off the station section offsets. My favorite method of doing this uses a plain staff or straightedge on which two points several feet apart that I will name A and B are marked. You must first draw the station line down over the hull or mark off whatever points you wish to take off along it. When doing this marking, you should hang a plumb bob off the sheer at the station locations as a guide to ensure that the station line and/or points are properly aligned and in the proper plane relative to one another. Once the marking is completed, take the staff and lean it in the same plane as the station, using the marks and a plumb bob as a guide, and measure from A and B to each point you want to take off. You need not be concerned to lean the staff in a consistent athwartship plane in taking off the various sections as long as it is kept consistent during each individual section measurement. (See Figure 11–3.)

This is such a simple and easy method for one person to use alone on hulls of all sizes that I have long used it exclusively for station sections. Any type rule can be used on small boats, but if you make fast two steel tapes at points A and B, and secure the staff in some way, you can scramble around on ladders or stagings to measure points on the largest of boats. To record these offsets, write the A and B measurements adjacent to one another for each point of each station. There is no way you can mix up the order or location of these offsets, since each pair can only meet at one point. Nor is the use of this triangulate system confined to taking off station sections. The staff can be propped up in the fore-and-aft centerline plane under bow and stern to take profile offsets. I have also picked up entire deck layouts, including the precise location of every hardware item, measuring from strategically placed A and B picks.

It should be noted that this method becomes less precise as the angle formed by the two lines at the point measured approaches either 0 or 180 degrees. Therefore, besides putting a good

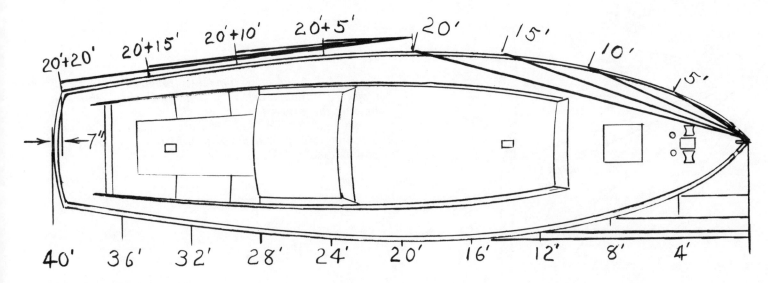

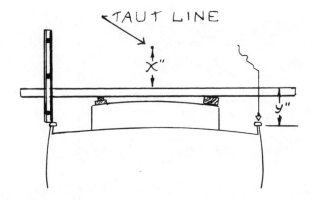

Top: Figure 11-1. *Methods of marking off station spacing for taking off lines. Port: Stations marked off on deck. (Reconstruct with radii intersecting half-breadths.) Starboard: Stations marked off from grid set up off boat.*

Right: Figure 11-2. *Beam measured on stick with level or plumb bob. Sheer heights can be taken at the same time by adding y inches (sheer to measuring stick) to x inches (measuring stick to taut reference line). Used in such a manner, a taut line is very handy as a base height or a point of reference.*

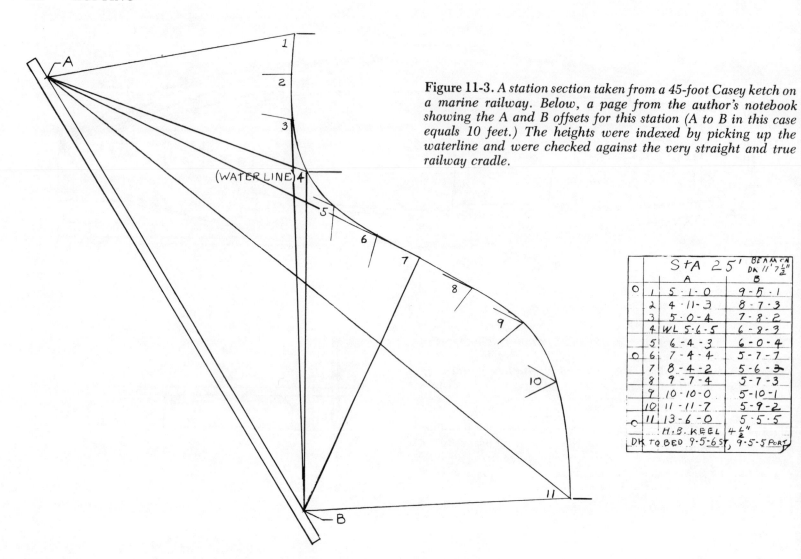

Figure 11-3. *A station section taken from a 45-foot Casey ketch on a marine railway. Below, a page from the author's notebook showing the A and B offsets for this station (A to B in this case equals 10 feet.) The heights were indexed by picking up the waterline and were checked against the very straight and true railway cradle.*

		STA 25'	BEAM ON DK 11' 7½"
		A	B
○	1	5 · 1 · 0	9 - 5 - 1
	2	4 · 11 · 3	8 - 7 - 3
	3	5 · 0 · 4	7 - 8 · 2
	4	WL 5 · 6 · 5	6 - 8 · 3
	5	6 - 4 · 3	6 - 0 · 4
○	6	7 - 4 · 4	5 - 7 - 7
	7	8 - 4 · 2	5 - 6 - 3
	8	9 - 7 · 4	5 - 7 · 3
	9	10 · 10 · 0	5 - 10 · 1
	10	11 · 11 · 7	5 - 9 · 2
○	11	13 - 6 · 0	5 · 5 · 5
		H. B. KEEL	4½"
	DK TO BED 9 · 5 · 6 ST	,	9 · 5 · 5 PORT

distance between A and B, you are better off to place the staff in an attitude relative to the line being taken off that will avoid very small or large angles. Though it is not often necessary if you have placed the staff carefully in the first place, you always have the option to move it to a better vantage point and take another set of offsets if you feel that the first set has given you poor definition in some area.

When you have taken off the station sections, the biggest single part of the job is done. Only the stem, stern, possibly some orientation offsets, and some part of the profile are needed to complete the lines plan. But to clarify the interrelation of the various items needed, let's say we have just taken nine stations off a 32-foot boat, that is, seven stations roughly four feet apart and a half station between each end and the nearest station. Exactly what else do you need?

• These stations must be located and keyed to each other in order to fix their locations on the hull so they can be drawn in their proper relationships. Much of this will have already been done in locating the stations on the boat in the first place. The lengthwise locations can be taken care of by using the distance from the bow perpendicular that each station was measured at.

The heights of the sections can be fixed by using the height of the sheer if the sheer heights have been taken independently with reference to a level or a straight line or to the waterline. The section heights can also be fixed by locating the profile on the sections, if these have been taken with reference to some straight or level line.

To fix the sections' athwartship locations, you need the half-breadth of the sheer or deck at side. That will take care of the upper end. The lower end will be on the centerline for part of the profile, but where it has width, you will need that half-breadth too.

• You will need to take off at least the stem; and on all but the most canoe-bodied boats you will have to take off those profile parts where the stations are not connected by a fair line.

• You will need the aft ending of the lines, either a transom or more profile points if she happens to be a double-ender. (*See* Figure 11–5.)

If you satisfy the above three items in some way, you can take enough information back to the loft to draw the hull lines. Start with the reference line or lines first and then "hang" the station sections on them. It should be obvious that a straight line on the loft floor with A and B points spaced as they were on the staff can be used to reconstruct the sections. Just swing intersecting arcs from A and B, using the offsets of a given point as radii, to recreate the individual points of the sections.

However, the reconstruction in itself does not locate a section in its proper place in the body plan. It would if you had carefully positioned the staff heightwise and half-breadthwise in exactly the same relation to the centerline as it was when you took off each section. That would be so difficult and time consuming as to be not worthwhile, and besides, it's not necessary.

What *is* necessary is that the height of each section be indexed to a reference line and that its half-breadths at the sheer and bottom of the profile be known. This information allows you to correctly position the sections as to height and in relation to a common centerline. The least involved method of drawing the sections is to draw each section elsewhere in the loft using the offsets picked up by the staff, pick up a pattern of each section, and then fit them into the body plan by simple measurement.

However, if you wish to draw the section in place in the body plan, you must reconstruct the A and B staff in its proper location relative to the centerline and waterline planes of the boat. For each section you must go by the following procedure. First set out the sheer point and the reference line relative to those planes.

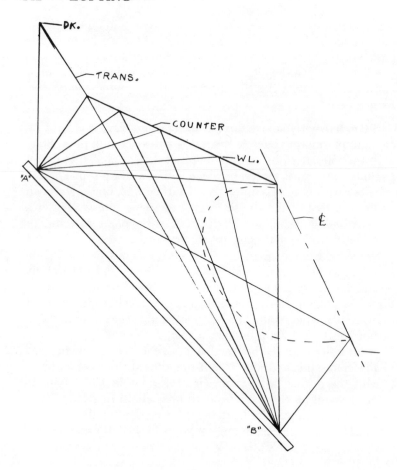

Figure 11-4. *Taking off the aft profile.*

Then locate points A and B at the intersections of arcs swung from the sheer and reference lines with their A and B offsets as radii. These two points will indicate how the staff was oriented when that particular section's offsets were taken off. You can then draw that section. You will have to repeat this procedure for each section, since it is likely that the angle of the staff was changed from station to station.

After the sections are drawn and the profile has been drawn, all you need to do is fair it all, and you have a boat. The rest depends upon your personal inclinations as to how much information you want. The particular boat may have some details that warrant lofting. For instance, you might want to take measurements for the rudder, propeller shaft angle, false piece, bow and stern sprits, masts, chainplates, the houses, hatches, and cockpit. Naturally, it all depends on whether you are interested only in the pure hull shape, or in the character of the boat, but this is all pretty simple once you have the lines.

Odds and Ends

At the risk of detaining potential lofters further, I will close this book by mentioning a few of the many unusual situations you are likely to encounter if you loft for any long period of time, as I have.

One problem the loftsman sometimes faces is laying down a boat that is too long for the available loft. One solution is to loft her in sections, a common practice in shipbuilding. If you do that, there should be a three-station overlap to fair the long lines through the break. The other solution for the too-long boat is to loft her to a smaller scale, perhaps one-half or one-third size. Scaled-down lofting works fine as long as you don't scale it down too much. Most unfairness can be seen pretty well down to about one-third of full-size. In fact, on very large boats, where it's sometimes hard for the eye to take in enough of a line at one time, the smaller scale can work to your advantage in judging the sweetness of a sheer and other prominent long lines. In order to make moulds you will have to draw the body plan full size; however, you do not have to draw this view at the smaller scale, just the profile and the half-breadth views. On the other hand, you will have to do full-size drawings of some parts in order to make patterns. This may seem like a lot of mental gear shifting, but that's all it is. Anyway, the mind is one of the most adaptable tools there is.

A few years ago I was in William "Billy" Lowell's boat shop where a 40-foot hull plug was being built. Due to a knee injury that prohibits him from crawling around on the floor, Billy lofts his boats to a smaller scale on the wall. This 40-footer's lofting was as crisp and fair as an October day and so was the plug. Having never seen anything quite like that before, I learned something that day.

One cannot work at lofting long before he is handed a plan and asked to lengthen, shorten, widen, narrow, or deepen it, or to make some other drastic change. I was once handed a plan and told to make the boat a foot narrower and a foot deeper. The designer wasn't lazy; the customer was in an all-fired hurry, and neither the designer nor I wanted to lose him. The changes were made on the floor and the offsets were sent back to the design office so that they could catch up and work out the rest of the design. These changes can be fun, because every loftsman is either a disappointed designer, or becomes one, but unless you know something about design and the type of boat involved, they are safer when they have the designer's blessing or when the builder has a "hold harmless" from the owner.

Still another probability in a loftsman's life is working with a set of offsets taken with metric measurements. That's no problem except for possibly having to look around for a metric rule and having to refresh yourself with the names and relationships of the units. The way to handle it is to jump right into the system and stay there until the job is done, and above all, to think metric. Don't try to convert, interpret, or interpolate. I once made over a foreign keel pattern after someone had made a mess of it trying to convert its metric offsets to inches and feet. This was back when metric rules were a curiosity in this country, but I found a small metric tape at a medical supply house, put my U.S. rules aside, and doctored the thing back to conformity with the millimeters indicated on the plan. I don't know to this day how big it was in our system, but what does that matter when it's right in its own language?

Before this book degenerates into interminable reminiscences that would increase its size exponentially without commensurate instruction, I had better end it with the sincere hope that the reader finds lofting as enjoyable as I have. And one last reminder—"A fair line supersedes any given measurement!"

Glossary

NOTE: The following is a list of words with which some readers may have trouble. The definition following each is not a dictionary-based one, but a "jargon of the trade"-type definition that describes the word's meaning as it is used in this book. (My understanding of some of these words may have a colloquial derivation not found in universal usage.)

Airex (trade name): One of the first and most successful PVC foams used in sandwich fiberglass construction.

Backbone: The centerline structure of a boat to which the frames and planking are attached in wooden construction.

Back Rabbet: The inside or back corner of the rabbet.

Bearding Line: The line where the inside of the planking intersects with the backbone members.

Bevel: An angle that is made when one surface meets another at any angle other than a right angle. A bevel of more than 90 degrees is a standing bevel, while a bevel of less than 90 degrees is an under bevel.

Body Plan: The lines plan that shows end views of a boat.

Bulkhead: A vertical partition in a hull's interior.

Buttock: In a lines plan, a vertical, lengthwise slice parallel to a boat's centerline.

Buttock Line: The line of the edge of a buttock.

Camber: A curvature, as in the deck.

C-Flex (trade name): A proprietary material used as a starting fiberglass layer on one-off fiberglass hulls and on parts built on open forms.

Chine: (1) A longitudinal angle or corner on the surface of a hull. (2) The member forming or backing the chine joint.

Cold-Molding: A method of boat construction in which two or more layers of thin planking strips are laid up over a mold or form and bonded with glue at room temperature.

Crossing: The intersection of two lines in a lines plan.

Crown: A radiused curve, especially that of a deck.

Designed Waterline: The plane at which the boat is designed to float.

Develop: To transform a curved, raked, or otherwise foreshortened view of a surface into a view where the surface is stretched out to its full dimensions.

Developable: A term that describes a curved shape to which flat sheets can be fitted without buckling.

Diagonal: In a lines plan, the edge of a fore-and-aft slice through the hull that is taken at an angle with the vertical centerline plane.

Draft: (1) The distance on a hull from the waterline to the lowest point of the keel. (2) The outward taper of a part and its mold at the upper, or open, end of the mold that makes for easier withdrawal of the part from the mold.

Expand: To draw out a part to its true dimensions from a foreshortened view.

Face: A surface of any part or member of a boat, usually designated as forward, aft, inboard, outboard, etc.

Fair: A term describing an even, regular line or shape.

False Stem: In a two-piece stem assembly, the facing that covers the ends of the planking.

Fid: A small piece or sample of a rib, planking, or other member used for tracing its thickness in the lofting or for fitting joints of one member to another, such as in a rabbet.

Floor: An athwartship member fitted on top of the keel and against the frames that acts like a web to strengthen the bottom for some distance across the centerline.

Form: The structure—usually a wooden framework of moulds and stringers—on which a hull or other part of a boat is built.

Frame: A rib or athwartship strengthening member to which the inside of the planking or skin is attached. This term is especially applicable to those that are sawn to shape.

Garvey: A boat with more or less rectangular sections and flat bow and stern transoms.

Grid: In a lines plan, the complex of straight lines on which the curved lines of any view are drawn. A given line will be a grid line in one view but may be a curved one in another.

GRP: Abbreviation for glass-reinforced plastic.

Half-Breadth: The distance normal to the centerline from it to any point on the outside of the boat.

Half-Breadth Plan: The lines plan that shows half of the hull split along the centerline as seen from above or below.

Height: A vertical measurement or offset.

Hood End: That end of a plank that meets up against the stem or the stern assembly.

Horn: To measure to like points on each side of a transverse member (or line) from a point forward or aft of it on the centerline to ensure that it is normal to the boat's centerline.

Horn Timber: The backbone member that runs from the top of the rudderpost to the stern. Sometimes called the after keel.

Inboard: Toward the center of a boat, or simply inside it.

Index: To key or mechanically establish the location of one part or piece in relation to another.

Keel: (1) The main backbone member of wooden vessels. (2) An integral underwater appendage found on both sailboats and powerboats.

Laminate: (1) (*verb*) To build up in layers. (2) (*noun*) The product so formed, also called a lamination.

Lapstrake: A method of planking in which one plank laps over the one below it.

Lift Strip: A ski-like inverted shelf along a high-speed powerboat's bottom.

List: To lean athwartships.

Long Lines: The lines that run along the length of a boat, especially the sheerline, waterlines, buttocks, and diagonals.

Mold: A form in or on which boats or parts are built.

Molded (dimension): The depth of a member taken normal to its top and bottom.

Mould: A frame, usually wooden, whose outline is the cross-sectional shape of a boat at a certain point.

Normal: Square with, or at 90 degrees to, a line or surface.

Offset: A measurement to a given point on the lines plan of a boat. The many offsets of a boat usually appear in a table called the table of offsets.

Ogee: A decorative curve often seen on the end of a coaming or rail that recurves to its original direction and then repeats itself.

One-off: A single boat built to a given design, as distinguished from a stock or production boat.

Outboard: Toward the outside of a boat, or simply outside of it.

Part: In fiberglass construction jargon, any molded part.

Parting Line: The line where the two sides of a split mold part.

Pickup Stick: A stick used to pick up offsets from the loft floor and set them off in another view or on a pattern or part.

Plug: A structure on which the mold for a boat or part is built.

Pram: A blunt-ended small boat having a bow transom.

Production Boat: A boat that is built as part of a series of similar units.

Profile: The lines plan that shows a side view of a boat.

Project: To carry a point or points from one view to another normal to some line of reference.

Rabbet: A notch in one piece of wood into which another fits, as the notch in backbone members into which the planking fits.

Rake: A slant off the vertical.

Release: To separate a part from its mold.

Rib: An athwartship member to which planking is fastened. This term refers especially to those that are bent to shape.

Ribband: Longitudinal strips of wood fastened across moulds or frames to hold them in line. When set up over moulds alone, the ribs are bent to them.

Rotated View: A view of a part that shows it as if it were rotated—usually 90 degrees—from its true orientation in the plan.

Run: The after part of a hull's underbody.

Scantlings: The dimensions of a boat's construction members.

Scribe: To transfer with dividers or a block of wood and pencil the shape of a surface to the face of a member that must fit up against that surface.

Scrive Board: A board or platform on which a body plan is drawn and moulds or frames assembled.

Section: A slice through the hull, particularly an athwartship slice. Often used when referring to the line that defines the edge of a section.

Set up: (*verb*) To erect the frame or form of a boat or plug.

Setup: (*noun*) The framework on which a boat is built.

Sheer: The line of the top of the hull along the side; also, a reference to the shape of that line, as in "curved," "straight," or "reverse."

Sided (dimension): The width of a member normal to its sides.

Sight Level: A simplified transit useful for measuring heights or striking a level line.

Standard View: Any of the three views in which boat plans are usually presented. These consist of profile, half-breadth (or plan view), and body plan.

Station: A reference location along a hull's length at which height and breadth measurements are taken and at which a cross-section is drawn in the body plan.

Station Line: A line normal to the fore-and-aft centerline of a station and the line of the edge of that cross-section in any view.

Stem: The backbone member to which the planking is attached at the bow.

Stringer: (1) A strip of wood bent longitudinally over moulds and/or bulkheads to support the skin or planking, either permanently or temporarily. (2) A longitudinal strip of any material on the inside of a boat's skin that stiffens the hull.

Sweep: A long curve.

Tabbing: Fiberglass laid up across a joint to tie two parts together.

Tooling: The plugs, molds, forms, or jigs used in building production boats.

Transit: A surveying instrument consisting of a telescope mounted on a tripod, equipped with leveling bubble, both horizontal and vertical pivots, and cross hairs; used for measuring heights and angles.

Transom: The flat or curved surface that is the after termination of a hull.

True View: A view that has the correct dimensions and shape of a part.

Water Level: A device consisting of a water source-attached hose with a sight glass or clear section at the other end through which one can see the water's level. A level line may be struck or heights measured from the water's level as the sight glass is carried about.

Waterline: The level at which a vessel sits in the water. In a lines plan, a horizontal slice through the hull or the line at the edge of such a slice.

Index